Toward a More Amicable Asia-Pacific Region

Japan's Roles

Edited by Yoneyuki Sugita

University Press of America,® Inc.
Lanham • Boulder • New York • Toronto • Plymouth, UK

Copyright © 2016 by University Press of America,® Inc.
4501 Forbes Boulevard, Suite 200, Lanham, Maryland 20706
UPA Acquisitions Department (301) 459-3366

Unit A, Whitacre Mews, 26-34 Stannary Street,
London SE11 4AB, United Kingdom

Library of Congress Control Number: 2015950951
ISBN: 978-0-7618-6678-7 (cloth : alk. paper)—ISBN: 978-0-7618-6679-4 (electronic)

♾️™ The paper used in this publication meets the minimum requirements of American
National Standard for Information Sciences Permanence of Paper for Printed Library
Materials, ANSI/NISO Z39.48-1992.

Contents

Acknowledgments

This book is a product of a series of international symposiums held at Osaka University in 2014 and 2015 financed by Osaka University International Joint Research Promotion Program, Osaka University International Symposium Grant, Osaka University International Joint Meetings Grant, and Grants-in-Aid for Scientific Research by Japan Society for the Promotion of Science. The editor, Yoneyuki Sugita, has also been supported by the Research Support System of Osaka University.

Introduction

Yoneyuki Sugita, Professor,
Osaka University

The Asia-Pacific region has been enjoying fast growing economy. As President Barack Obama's "pivot to Asia" strategy indicates, this region is an engine for the world economic growth. However, the Asia-Pacific has also been an unstable region suffering from many sources of conflicts such as the dispute over the Senkaku/Diaoyu Islands, the unsettled Exclusive Economic Zone (EEZ) borders, North Korean nuclear issues, and many others. Do we need a hegemonic power to stabilize this region? What can we do to deal with the rapid emergence of China? How can we deal with anti-Japanese feelings in this region? Is there any way to deal with the problem of the Senkaku/Diaoyu Islands? How can we analyze the nuclear crisis on the Korean peninsula? Can the European Union make any contribution to stabilizing the Asia-Pacific region? Those are some of the concrete questions this book tackles with in order to find ways and means to establish a more amicable Asia-Pacific region.

In Chapter 1, dealing with U.S.-Japan relations from the 1945 through the 1990s, Yoneyuki Sugita addresses why the structural realists' prediction that the U.S.-Japan alliance would inevitably weaken or vanish has not been realized over the two decades since the end of the Cold War. He concludes that a more amicable U.S.-Japan relationship was established in the demise of the Cold War because the United States succeeded in creating a dynamic in East Asia that was similar to the one created during the Cold War.

In Chapter 2, Professor Miyuki Daimaruya explores a mechanism by which a more amicable relationship was established within the United States between the U.S. government and Japanese American *Nisei* (second-generation Japanese) in the Korean War (1950-1953), featuring a female soldier's case and revealing how *Nisei* military service affected a personal life in the post-WWII period. For all *Nisei* soldiers, the Korean War was a significant moment because it was the first war in which Niseis participated in racially integrated units. The U.S. government welcomed *Nisei* service in Korea because they could represent loyal *racial minorities* showing both anti-communism and a symbol of domestic racial integration in the United States.

In Chapter 3, Professor Victor Teo seeks a way to build a more amicable Sino-Japanese relationship by reexamining three important assumptions that are commonly made. First, China is often assumed to be Japan's number one challenge in the foreseeable future. Second, the United States alliance's with Japan is the entire answer to Japan's vast array of foreign and security problems. Third, the maintenance of US-Japan alliance necessarily precludes Japan from working together with China. Professor Teo makes three arguments. First, Japan's foreign policy challenges lie in managing her relations not only with China but also the United States. The United States remains a problem as much as it is a solution for Japan's foreign policy in the long run. Second, it is entirely possible for both Japan and China to work together under certain circumstances. Third, East Asia can only become a more harmonious region if and only if Chinese and Japanese politicians consider the stakes more carefully than what they have done in previous years.

In Chapter 4, Professor Reinhard Drifte analyzes approaches to resolving the disputes in the East China Sea. The author addresses the unsettled Exclusive Economic Zone (EEZ) borders between Japan and China, China and South Korea, and Japan and South Korea, as well as the territorial dispute over the Senkaku/Diaoyu Islands. All four issues are to various degrees interdependent. In the case of the territorial dispute, he proposes several steps, such as, a new shelving agreement of the dispute, Confidence and Security Building Measures, joint exploitation of marine resources, and finally addressing the sovereignty issue through internationalization or sovereignty sharing. In order to arrive at a new shelving agreement, he investigates why the 1972 and 1978 shelving agreement failed and what lessons have to be learned to achieve a more sustainable agreement.

In Chapter 5, Professor David Walton seeks to find ways to realize more amicable relations between Australia and Japan and Australia and China, especially Australia's response to the rapid rise of China. He argues that there is no likelihood of a substantial rupture or change in Australian relations with Japan and China in the short-term; however, these relations in the mid to long-term will depend on a range of variables. He concludes that current Australian policies including a genuine engagement with China while maintaining a close security alliance with the United States and developing closer security ties with Japan suggest that Australia, like most countries in the Asia Pacific, will be pursuing a hedging strategy for the foreseeable future.

In Chapter 6, Professor Emilian Kavalski examines whether there are normative powers in the Asia-Pacific as a way to make it a more amicable region. He contends that normative powers are those actors that are recognized as such by others, indicating that the definitions of the 'normal' are not merely undertaken by normative power, but that they emerge in the context of its interaction with others. He examines this proposition by undertaking parallel assessment of normative power Europe, normative power China, and normative power Japan. This comparison leads to elicit the key elements of normative power not only in the Asia-Pacific, but in global life in general.

In Chapter 7, Professor Bart Gaens explicates ways to build a more amicable relationship between the European Union and Asia focusing on the Asia-Europe Meeting (ASEM). ASEM is a summit-level yet informal dialogue forum aiming to advance interregional relations between Europe and Asia in the political, economic and socio-cultural fields. Examining the features and changing contours of ASEM as an international institution, he demonstrates the fragmented nature of Europe-Asia cooperation, reveals the limits to the EU's ambitions to play a stronger role in the East Asian region, and looks ahead to the future of interregional relations. Professor Gaens adds that an international institution such as ASEM is an important signpost reflecting changes in global governance in general and in regionalist projects in particular.

With these seven chapters, we hope to provide thoughts and analyses to lead to a more amicable Asia-Pacific region.

Chapter One

U.S.-Japan Relations in Transition

From Cold War to Post-Cold War

Yoneyuki Sugita, Professor,
Osaka University

The demise of the Cold War had a significant impact on the relationship between the United States and Japan, but not in the way structural realists imagined. In 1993, Kenneth Waltz argued that Japan would try to achieve a greater balance of power with the United States, or at least seek strategic independence after the demise of the Cold War.[1] Such actions would cause the U.S.-Japan alliance to inevitably weaken or vanish altogether. George Friedman and Meredith LeBard went further to envisage that the United States and Japan would wage war in the post-Cold War period.[2]

In the two decades since the end of the Cold War, however, Japan still has not acted as these structural realists predicted. This chapter seeks to explain why these predictions were not realized by tracing the continuity and discontinuity of U.S.-Japan relations both during and after the Cold War. In doing so, this chapter positions Japan's post-Cold War security policy within the broader context of post-World War II U.S.-Japan security relations. A hypothesis is that since the end of the Cold War, the United States has succeeded in creating a dynamic in the Asia-Pacific region that is similar to the one created during the Cold War. This is why both the United States and Japan have found it beneficial to maintain the U.S.-Japan alliance, even in the post-Cold War period. This chapter seeks to verify this hypothesis.

In not fulfilling the predictions of the structural realists, Japan strengthened its image as an anomalous and unique state after World War II; however, an increasing number of scholars note that, in the post-Cold War era, Japan has been making efforts to transform itself from an anomalous country

into a "normal country." These scholars claim that Japan's active foreign and
security policies have been developed in response to factors such as a growing regional threat from China and North Korea, political changes and administrative reforms that have drastically increased the Japanese prime minister's power, and changes in Japanese people's perception of their country's
role in the international community.[3]

Other scholars have offered a variety of interpretations as to why the
counterbalancing against the United States did not take place. Stephen Walt
introduces the concept of "balance of threat" in place of "balance of power"[4]
in order to explain why major powers do not ally against the United States.
The balance of threat theory primarily focuses on threats instead of focusing
exclusively on power units such as military or offensive capabilities. The
assumption is that "states that are viewed as aggressive are likely to provoke
others to balance against them."[5] Furthermore, as Susanne Klien argues, for
Japan, the demise of the Cold War increased the danger of abandonment by
the United States. For Klien, it was the constant fear of international isolation
that made Japan stick to the U.S.-Japan alliance in the post-Cold War era, as
the alliance gave Japan psychological confirmation of its integration into the
international system.[6] Similarly, David Arase claims that the United States'
new position as leader of the post-Cold War world's unipolar structure gave
it greater freedom to abandon Japan. As a result, Tokyo struggled to change
its security policies, as it was focused on maintaining its alliance with the
United States.[7] William C. Wohlforth asserts that U.S. power has been so
preponderant in the post-Cold War era that no rational country is willing to
provoke the United States by counterbalancing.[8] Indeed, Thomas Risse
argues that it is because liberal and capitalist democracies are currently responsible for establishing and maintaining global order that the current world
is not in a state of anarchy. This explains the lack of counterbalancing against
the United States by Japan or any other powerful country.[9] Within the context of these arguments, a Japan that maintains and even tries to strengthen its
alliance with the United States is not an anomaly, but is acting in a perfectly
rational manner.

Takafumi Ohtomo contends that, because Japan is aware that other Asian
countries might see it as a potential threat, it has maintained its alliance with
the United States in order to allay the fear and suspicions of its neighbors that
it might revert to war-like behavior.[10] Paul Midford considers Japan's constrained security policy as a rational reassurance strategy preventing its East
Asian neighbors from ganging up against it.[11] While Japan has certainly
considered its neighbors' concerns about its resurgence, its foreign and security policies have targeted its relationship with the United States. Consequently, it is necessary to pay more attention to U.S.-Japan relations.

When analyzing Japan's foreign and security policies over the long term,
many scholars highlight the consistency in the post-World War II era. Jenni-

fer M. Lind finds this consistency to be a buck-passing strategy that seeks to transfer to the United States the costly job of balancing against regional threats in Asia. Lind believes that Japan will never make the military contribution to its own security that the United States would like unless Washington reduces its military presence in East Asia, or Japan's threat environment significantly worsens.[12] However, since Japan has been accepting a greater security role in the post-Cold War period, instead of just passing the buck to the United States, this does not entirely explain Japan's behavior.

Offering an alternative explanation, constructivists, such as Peter J. Katzenstein, Nobuo Okawara, and Thomas U. Berger, characterize Japan as having an antimilitarist norm that has consistently influenced its security policies both during and after the Cold War. They focus on the normative structures, identities, and the culture of antimilitarism in Japan, arguing that Japan has implemented pragmatic adjustments to changes in the international environment, constrained its security policy, and channeled its foreign policy in a liberal direction.[13] Indeed, norms, identities, and culture are critical factors shaping Japan's foreign and security policies. However, since these intangible factors tend to be consistent, they might not be useful for explaining structural changes between the Cold-War period and the post-Cold War period.

Yoshihide Soeya characterizes Japan's postwar security policy as the product of the nation's de facto "middle-power" diplomacy. A middle power is a nation that is influential in economic or certain strategic aspects, but that does not aspire to become a great military power willing to use force as a normative policy instrument. According to Soeya, incremental changes to Japanese post-Cold War security policies consolidated, rather than fundamentally altered, the foundation of this de facto middle-power security policy.[14] Kenneth Pyle claims that Japan has consistently and skillfully been able to adapt to changes in the international system. As in the past, Pyle believes, Japan is less likely to take the initiative in creating a new international order and spreading its value and vision, but more likely to remain a cautious adapter to the changing external environment.[15] While both Soeya and Pyle emphasize the continuity of Japan's foreign and security policies in the post-Cold War period, there have also been important changes. Consequently, in order to have a better understanding of how the demise of the Cold War has affected U.S.-Japan relations, it is necessary to analyze what has remained unchanged and what has changed in the post-Cold War period.

Japan has not been alone in its adaptation. The United States, too, has made efforts to adjust the U.S.-Japan alliance to the changing external environment since the demise of the Cold War. In turn, these adjustments have driven Japan to not act as the structural realists predicted. The following sections seek to verify the hypothesis that, in the post-Cold War period, the United States has established a dynamic in East Asia consisting of three primary elements explained below. This dynamic is similar to the one created during the Cold War, and it is because of this post-Cold War dynamic in East Asia that Japan has found it rational and beneficial to maintain and strengthen the U.S.-Japan alliance.

U.S.-JAPAN RELATIONS BETWEEN 1945 AND 1989

In the 45 years following World War II, two key factors helped maintain relative stability in the world: (a) fear of the communist threat, and (b) the existence of a hegemon, the United States. On the one hand, by constantly evoking the threat of "the other" (in the figure of the Soviet Union) and the existence of an East-West conflict, the United States was able to achieve unity in the Western bloc. On the other hand, the United States provided its allies in the Western bloc with economic support, a military shield, and a sense of relief. These positive benefits also contributed to the stability of the postwar world. During this period, Japan was able to take advantage of the U.S. military shield without wasting resources, utilizing its status as a feeble ally in an unstable area surrounded by two giant communist countries—the Soviet Union and the People's Republic of China (PRC)—and its economic vulnerability.[16]

As for East Asia, the United States began to take a deep interest in the economic and political conditions of the region in the post-World War II era. Scholars tend to assume that the Cold War conditions centered in Europe merely extended to East Asia.[17] They seek to explain U.S.-East Asian relations primarily through this Cold War lens. Closer examination of postwar U.S.-Japan relations, however, suggests that the Cold War perspective has limited explanatory power. For example, although Japan was surrounded by powerful communist countries, the United States did not force it to implement a rapid and large-scale rearmament to deal with the communist threat. Furthermore, the United States and the Soviet Union seemed to have a tacit agreement to maintain a status quo in China's civil war in the late 1940s.[18]

While the Cold War perspective focuses primarily on the East-West confrontation, the Cold War period coincided with the period of U.S. hegemony in the Western bloc. A definition of hegemony starts with one state having a preponderance of power along with a full spectrum of economic resources, namely, manufacturing, science/technology, and finance. The hegemony is possible largely because the hegemonic power has military superiority and an uncontestable ability to define international political, institutional, ideological, and legal norms.[19] Applying a hegemonic perspective involves not only studying the East-West clash as a *sui generis* topic, but also examining how conflicts between allies within each bloc are managed. As a hegemonic power, the main postwar goal of the United States was to construct a stable global system premised on a multilateralist approach to the global division of labor and trade. As for U.S.-Japan relations, because of Japan's geographic proximity to both the Soviet Union and the PRC and strong economic ties with the PRC, the United States feared that Japan might be easily lured by these communist countries. Consequently, the United States sought to make itself more attractive to Japan.

At the same time, the United States developed a prejudiced perception of Japan, and Asia in general, which gave a unique character to U.S.-Japan relations. The United States inadvertently employed condescending attitudes in its dealings with Japan. The United States tended to underestimate Japan's powers of resistance in the face of communism partly because of the American preconception of Asian backwardness.

In sum, three important factors influenced postwar U.S.-Japan relations: (a) fear of the communist threat, (b) the United States as a hegemonic power, and (c) the United States' prejudiced view of Japan. These three factors were not mutually exclusive, but intricately comingled to affect the U.S.-Japan bilateral relationship. In the next section, this chapter explains how these three factors affected U.S.-Japan relations between 1945 and 1989, and then goes on to explicate how these factors transformed in the 1990s.

Fear of the Communist Threat

Constantly dangling the threatening "other" (the Soviet Union) in Japan's face was an effective tactic for the United States to achieve its desired form of unity in U.S.-Japan relations. The existence of the East-West conflict essentially gave the United States the opportunity to manage Japan's behaviors in the international arena and keep Japan in the Western bloc.

The United States felt that it was imperative to resist the spread and expansion of communism in Asia. To this end, it was necessary to make Japan a bulwark against communism, and so the U.S.-Japan security treaty was concluded with two major pillars: Japan's rearmament and the stationing of U.S. military forces in Japan. Japan was reluctant to implement a rapid, large-scale rearmament. The United States, too, was ambivalent about Japan's remilitarization, placing top priority on maintaining its military bases and stationing its armed forces in Japan. A U.S. presence in Japan was designed to protect Japan, to use it as a springboard to ensuring peace and stability in the Asia-Pacific region, and to manage Japan's remilitarization. Fear of the communist threat combined with U.S. pressure gave the Japanese people no choice but to endure the installment of U.S. bases and armed forces in Japan.

The United States as a Hegemonic Power

If the threat of the "other" provided some incentive for Japan to stay in the Western bloc, the economic and security benefits offered by the United States, a hegemonic power, were even more attractive. Charles Spinks of General Headquarters (GHQ) in occupied Japan recognized, "[The] Japanese are essentially realists and their present general tendency to seek or accept an orientation toward the United States is inspired more by pragmatic considerations than any innate or compelling affection for the United States."[20] During the allied occupation of Japan, GHQ controlled Japan's foreign trade and exempted Japan from the heavy burden of its huge trade deficit, much of which was underwritten by American aid. U.S. assistance amounted to $404 million in 1947 and $461 million in 1948, accounting for 92 percent of Japanese imports in 1947 and 75 percent in 1948.[21] U.S. economic assistance to Japan continued in various ways after the occupation.[22]

In the early post-World War II period, Japan struggled in its economic recovery, and the Central Intelligence Agency (CIA) predicted that Japan's "pro-Western orientation [would last] at least during the next two or three years." Economic prosperity, however, would be essential if this orientation were to be maintained: "If, however, Japan is unable to solve its economic problems, it will be particularly vulnerable to economic and diplomatic pressures from the Soviet Bloc and will be tempted to seize opportunities for closer economic and political relations with the [Soviet] Bloc."[23] The CIA concluded that the United States would need to meet two conditions in order to retain Japan on its side: the maintenance of Japan's security and the assurance of its economic prosperity.[24] In order to achieve these objectives, the United States had to establish an ongoing process of policymaking with regard to Japan.

Japan experienced a large trade deficit throughout the 1950s due to the Korean War, which broke out in June 1950. The war sparked a sudden economic boom in Japan, making its imports much greater than its exports.[25] However, large special procurements from the United States financed the trade deficit and restored a favorable balance of international payments. These special procurements jumped from $149 million (53.64 billion yen) in 1950 to $824 million (296.64 billion yen) in 1952. The amounts then declined to $809 million (291.24 billion yen) and $596 million (214.56 billion yen) in 1953 and 1954 respectively, but annual procurements continued to amount to roughly $500 million (180 billion yen) per year on average until 1961.[26] After the end of World War II, Japan suffered from trade losses amounting to $287 million, $408 million, $790 million, and $427 million in 1951, 1952, 1953, and 1954 respectively.[27] The special procurements covered these trade losses, greatly contributing to Japan's economic recovery and growth.

The Cold War offered Japan favorable international conditions: Japan's economic recovery and the integration of Japan into the Western bloc became major objectives for the United States. Consequently, Washington provided Japan with access to U.S. markets as well as opportunities to transfer technology easily from the United States and permitted Japanese restrictions against imports and investments.[28] In the 1950s, the fundamental assumption of the Eisenhower administration was that creating people of plenty in the world by expansion of the economic pie would be the best measure to contain the social pressure for economic redistribution and protectionism at home and abroad. The Eisenhower administration successfully applied this assumption to Japan and kept the country in the Western bloc.[29]

American-led financial institutions also aided Japan's economic recovery. During the 1950s and 1960s, when Japan needed a large amount of capital for its economic recovery and development, the International Bank for Reconstruction and Development (the World Bank) and the Export-Import Bank of Washington provided Japan with long-term, low-interest credits.[30] In addition, the United States opened its domestic market to Japan's less competitive goods in order to promote Japan's economic recovery and growth. Indeed, the United States' global economic strategy of establishing a free, liberal, multilateral trade system resulted in the opening of the U.S. domestic market to Japanese goods. Meanwhile, Japan was able to gain the latest technology from America.[31] As a result of these developments, Japan acquired advanced country status in the General Agreement on Tariffs and Trade (GATT) in 1963. Japan was also inducted as a member of the "closed eight" of the International Monetary Fund (IMF) in 1964. In the same year, Japan became the first non-Western country to join the Organization for Economic Cooperation and Development (OECD).

The Vietnam War in the 1960s also generated special offshore procurement demands, which assisted Japanese economic growth in an indirect manner. The United States poured economic and military aid into South Vietnam and friendly neighboring Southeast Asian countries. These countries, in turn, used these aid grants to procure necessary goods from Japan. The statistics prepared by the Ministry of International Trade and Industry indicate that although the Vietnam special procurement amounted to less than 10 percent of the entire export value, its contribution ratio to the export increase in Japan surpassed 50 percent in the late 1960s.[32] Altogether, U.S. hegemony provided Japan with a free and liberal trade system, the U.S. domestic market, and special procurements, which were all instrumental to Japan's economic recovery and growth.

The United States' Prejudiced View of Japan

The American fear of communism in the postwar era fostered an anti-communist outlook, causing a psychic crisis that can be partly attributed to the historical development of American society. America began in the modern age without the experience of feudalism. Consequently, it was difficult for Americans to appreciate the diverse routes that could lead to social development (e.g., feudalism, absolutism, and socialism). As a result, Americans developed a disdain for those belief systems, valorizing liberal society as an absolute universal good. In particular, communism's disavowal of the market economy and promotion of authoritarian forms of state social control were two principles directly opposed to American core values. In effect, anti-communism became a fortunate device that Americans could use to reaffirm the legitimacy of their own society. [33]

Americans feared that communism would spread like a virus to vulnerable parts of the globe. Washington policymakers instinctively perceived East Asia as one of the most unstable regions in the world and a place where communism could easily make inroads. The United States held a condescending view of East Asia as a "pre-modern society" and regarded the region as a passive entity that desired the strong leadership of the United States. Washington suspected that it was impossible for liberal democracy, market principles, and other rational modes of thinking to suddenly spring forth in the region from under the weight of centuries of Asian backward traditions. In Washington's view, these traditions boiled down to a respect for power, authority, and prestige. Accordingly, Americans did not trust that Asians would or could voluntarily adopt liberal capitalism, and even eyed the pro-U.S. inclinations among many postwar Japanese people with suspicion, believing that the seemingly friendly Japanese attitude was fickle in light of that country's long history of authoritarianism.

Anticipating confrontation against the Soviet Union, the U.S. military expected to utilize Japan's military potential. As early as 1946, the U.S. military considered using Japan's military potential to win a future war against the Soviet Union. [34] However, Japan's shaky economy prevented the United States from pursuing this option. In addition, Washington was reluctant to let Japan control its own military future by allowing the country to independently implement its rearmament. Many U.S. officials regarded Japanese rearmament as risky, if not dangerous. In short, because of this distrust of Japan, the United States was in dilemma: Washington wanted to see a strong and rearmed Japan as a bulwark against communism, while at the same time it feared that a rearmed Japan might defect to the Communist bloc. In July 1949, the CIA emphasized the unpredictable consequences of Japanese rearmament: "Even if Japan's military defenses were re-established ... there would be no assurance that those forces would be used in opposition to

Communism, if there were compelling economic reasons for an accommodation with the Communist world." Apart from trust issues, the probable negative reactions to Japan's rearmament on the part of Japan's former enemies also had to be acknowledged. This led the CIA to conclude that the "reluctance of former enemies to permit a Japanese military renascence will probably preclude Japan's complete defensive self-sufficiency for at least the next twenty years."[35]

Once China fell into communist hands in October 1949, Japan became the only power in East Asia that could function as a reliable ally for the United States. However, because Japan was an undependable former enemy, the United States continued to fear that Japan might pursue neutralist policies and try to play the United States against the Soviet Union. Washington could not simply trust Tokyo's good will; it had to stimulate Japan's self-interest to side with the Western bloc by providing Japan with economic prosperity, that is, by convincing the Japanese government that allying with the United States would be economically beneficial for Japan.[36]

The Korean War seemed to change this trend. General Douglas MacArthur, the Supreme Commander for the Allied Powers (SCAP), issued a directive to the Japanese Government on July 8, 1950, establishing a Police Reserve Force of 75,000 troops and increasing the Maritime Safety Force by 8,500 troops. The U.S. military also emphasized the necessity of Japanese rearmament, especially following U.S. President Harry S. Truman's decision to further deplete U.S. forces in Asia by dispatching four additional divisions to Europe.[37]

Nevertheless, Washington officials were not sure how far they could go to pressure Japan into rapid and large-scale rearmament. In July 1950, John Foster Dulles, Special Consultant to the Secretary of State, reported to Paul Nitze, Director of the Policy Planning Staff (PPS) of the State Department, that Japanese rearmament at that precise moment "would encounter serious and understandable objections on the part of former victims of Japanese aggression and, indeed, from the Japanese themselves."[38] General MacArthur also stated that the Allied Powers continued to be more concerned about the threat of a remilitarized Japan than the threat of an attack on Japan.[39] The best solution, therefore, was to station U.S. armed forces in Japan, thereby putting the United States in the position to manage Japan's military activity. However, the stationing of troops in Japan was a sensitive measure that always had the potential to violate Japan's sovereignty.

As a weak ally in an unstable area surrounded by two giant communist countries, Japan discovered that its weakness was its best asset for dealing with the United States. The fact that the United States did not trust Japan laid the groundwork for the so-called Yoshida Doctrine, which saw the Japanese government allocating as many resources as possible to economic recovery and as few as possible to rearmament. The Japanese government's primary task was to find the absolute minimum defense contribution that would not damage the U.S.-Japan alliance. In order to resist the U.S. pressure for rearmament, Japanese leaders often evoked Article Nine—a war-renouncing clause in the new Japanese constitution—Japan's antimilitarist norm, the emergence of left-wing forces, and Japan's vulnerability to communist infiltration. Moreover, Washington could not push Japan too hard concerning its rearmament program, fearing that this topic might exacerbate the sensitive issue of U.S. bases in Japan. Washington had to continue providing Japan with security and economic prosperity, while being careful not to make the security issue into a subject of hot political debate in the Diet and among the Japanese people. Partly because of American prejudice against Japan and the Japanese people, the United States stationed its armed forces in Japan after the Allied occupation, but Japan made the best use of this development in order to implement its constrained rearmament.

In sum, between 1945 and 1989, U.S.-Japan relations were generally defined by three factors: fear of the communist threat, the United States' position as a hegemonic power, and the United States' prejudiced view of Japan. The next section explains what happened when the Cold War ended.

U.S.-JAPAN RELATIONS IN THE 1990S

The 45-year Cold War may be considered the period of "long peace."[40] Consequently, in the 1990s, the world was faced with a double crisis in the wake of the Cold War, as it lost the two key stabilizing factors of the postwar era: American hegemony and the Cold War.[41] First, American hegemony began to decline in the late 1960s. Because of the high costs of the Vietnam War and increased domestic spending, the United States suffered from inflation, a balance-of-payments deficit, and a trade deficit. In 1971, President Richard Nixon unilaterally canceled the direct convertibility of the U.S. dollar to gold, essentially ending the Bretton-Woods system of international financial exchange. The United States was no longer able to provide Japan with a sense of economic protection. To America's surprise, Japan emerged as an economic rival, and the two countries fought fierce trade wars throughout the 1980s.

The second stabilizing factor, the Cold War, came to an end with the Malta Summit in December 1989 and the dismantling of the Soviet Union in December 1991. In the aftermath, the United States closed about 60 percent of its overseas bases.[42] . The U.S. Congress also undertook a complete review of the U.S. strategy in East Asia, demanding a reduction of U.S. military forces. To meet this demand, the National Security Council issued its annual report in March 1990, stating that the United States would implement disarmament in Asia by 12–13 percent.[43] In 1990, the United States had about 135,000 troops stationed in East Asia. This new plan called for a phased reduction of the U.S. military forces in the region, decreasing the number of troops by 15,250 by 1992 and to around 100,000 over a ten-year period. In September 1991, the George H.W. Bush administration announced its plan to withdraw its tactical nuclear weapons deployed overseas.[44] The U.S. military commitment in East Asia, thus, became much smaller after the demise of the Cold War.

As for Japan, as the Cold War restraint disappeared, Japan's relative autonomy increased. Japan began to reconsider the strategic role of the U.S.-Japan alliance and to devise independent strategies in East Asia. In a sense, this movement seemed to be in line with the structural realists' theory that Japan would move away from its alliance with the United States. However, the U.S. response to this development determined the future of Japanese autonomy. Facing a new international environment in the 1990s, the United States had to modify the U.S.-Japan alliance through three main measures: (a) orchestrating a pseudo-Cold War environment in East Asia, (b) seeking to establish a complementary U.S.-Japan relationship that would satisfy and manage Japan's more active role in the international arena, and (c) enacting measures sparked by the United States' prejudiced view of Japan.

Orchestrating a Pseudo-Cold War in East Asia

Japan found itself under pressure from various countries and international bodies to play a more significant political, military, and financial role in global affairs. Japan's policy toward North Korea was the most vivid representation of a new, more active post-Cold War foreign policy. In an attempt to establish itself as a post-Cold War regional leader in Asia, Tokyo took the initiative in attempting to construct a more amicable relationship with Pyongyang. Japan embarked on this approach with Prime Minister Noboru Takeshita's formal apology on March 30, 1989 for Japan's aggression during the Asia-Pacific War. In September 1990, Shin Kanemaru, a former Vice President of the Liberal Democratic Party (LDP), and Makoto Tanabe, Vice President of the Japan Socialist Party (JSP), led a team of Diet members (13 from the LDP and 9 from the JSP) to North Korea. They brought with them a letter from Prime Minister Toshiki Kaifu expressing a sincere apology for Japan's colonial rule over the Korean Peninsula and the desire to take the first step in establishing a friendly relationship.

During the Cold War, North Korea had displayed an interest in developing nuclear weapons and ballistic missiles. In the 1980s, North Korea had received financial assistance from Iran and other countries to develop Scud-B missiles. By the latter half of the decade, North Korea was exporting Scuds abroad. By 1989 (but possibly much earlier), analysis of photographic evidence gathered by U.S. intelligence clearly showed that North Korea had established domestic facilities capable of reprocessing nuclear fuel for use in developing nuclear weapons. Although this evidence pointed to the possibility of North Korea joining the club of countries possessing nuclear weapons, neither the United States nor anyone else did anything to bring this threat to the attention of the world. North Korea remained largely invisible behind the threat of the Soviet Union, and the United States paid little attention to the North Korean problem. [45]

Nevertheless, the United States was not happy with Japan's independent move toward reconciliation with North Korea. Although, up to that point, the United States had paid little attention to North Korea (with the brief exception of the Korean War), the importance of North Korea suddenly grew as it emerged as a suitable replacement for the former Soviet Union. [46] Because North Korea was a militarily and economically weak country, it was never seen as a serious threat to the United States. But given its geographic location, any crisis centered on North Korea could potentially be used to make South Korea and Japan more compliant to the United States, enabling the United States to more effectively manage the future behaviors of South Korea and Japan. [47]

On February 25, 1992, Robert Gates, CIA Director, testified to the House Foreign Affairs Committee that North Korea was a "few months to a couple of years" from becoming a nuclear power. [48] North Korea became an international hot spot in February 1993 when it denied a request from the International Atomic Energy Agency (IAEA) for agency inspectors to be permitted to examine nuclear waste-related sites near Yongbyon. North Korea's refusal immediately caused alarm and suspicion at the IAEA and in the capitals of some countries that Pyongyang was working toward the development of nuclear weapons. Suspicions about the possible existence of such a program reached their peak in March 1993, when North Korea announced its intention to withdraw from the Nuclear Non-Proliferation Treaty (NPT). In May 1993, North Korea fired a Nodong missile over Japan, and tension between the United States, Japan, and North Korea continued to increase over the subsequent 12 months.

President Bill Clinton considered preemptive military strikes on Yongbyon, where North Korea was allegedly developing its nuclear weapons, [49] but eventually rejected this idea because of the potential devastation such strikes might cause. U.S. General Gary Luck, former Commander of U.S. Forces Korea, estimated that a second Korean War would result in $1 trillion in damage and generate 1 million casualties. [50] Therefore, Washington had to come up with another solution to deal with the North Korean situation.

Japan, meanwhile, was interested in carving out a more active and independent role in the region. In August 1994, the Advisory Group on Defense Issues—the prime minister's private advisory group on Japan's security policy for the 21st century—submitted a report entitled "The Modality of the

Security and Defense Capability of Japan: The Outlook for the 21st Century"
(Higuchi Report) to Prime Minister Tomiichi Murayama. According to this
report, "Unlike in the European nations, … in the Asia/Pacific region the
collapse of the Soviet Union has not meant such a dramatic change in the
security environment. There is no evidence that the level of military tension
in this part of the world has rapidly declined." In other words, the demise of
the Soviet Union had not automatically established a peaceful and stable
order in the Asia-Pacific region. On the contrary, the Cold-War style of
threat continued, particularly in terms of "the tensions across the Demilitarized Zone in the Korean Peninsula." Under the assumption that "the United
States no longer holds an overwhelming advantage in terms of overall national strength," the report recommended that "Japan should extricate itself
from its security policy of the past that was, if anything, passive, and hence-
forth play an active role in shaping a new order. Indeed Japan has the responsibility of playing such a role." In order to accomplish this objective, the
report emphasized the "enhancement of the functions of the Japan-U.S. security relationship." However, this was prioritized as a second measure pre-
ceded by the "promotion of multilateral security cooperation on a global and
regional scale."[51] This report gave the impression that Japan sought to adopt
a more proactive posture in the post-Cold War era, shifting from the total
reliance on its bilateral alliance with the United States toward a multilateral
security arrangement.[52]

The Higuchi Report shocked Washington. Sensing Japan's desire to move
out of the U.S. orbit, the United States struggled to redefine the U.S.-Japan
alliance between August 1994 and February 1995. Citing the example of the
nuclear crisis in North Korea, the United States argued that conditions of
instability and threat, and a Cold War structure would persist in the Asia-
Pacific region, despite the collapse of the Soviet Union. In line with its
posture of global military preparedness and quick response (i.e., using a
flexible array of options to react to developments in international hot spots).
The United States emphasized the view that the U.S.-Japan alliance and the
maintenance of forward-deployed forces were important for securing the
regional balance of power in East Asia and for defusing new and emerging
local threats.[53] Concerns about stability and various other problems were
framed by the recognition that the Asia-Pacific region had the greatest economic growth potential of any other region in the world. In light of these
issues, both countries were convinced that a U.S. military presence was
indispensable to ensuring regional security, stability, and growth. Thus, they
concluded that it was critical to maintain the U.S.-Japan alliance.

The United States tried to make the best use of North Korea's threat in
order to contain independent Japanese foreign and security policies. In a bid
to ease regional tensions, in October 1994, the United States negotiated the
"Agreed Framework" (the Geneva Agreement) with North Korea, according

to which Pyongyang agreed to "freeze its graphite-moderated reactors and related facilities,"[54] halting any further production of plutonium. Moreover, North Korea agreed to accept IAEA inspections once it concluded a contract with the United States providing North Korea with two 1,000 megawatt light-water reactors. In return, the United States formed an international consortium tasked with building the light-water reactors by 2003 and also agreed to provide North Korea with 500,000 tons of heavy fuel oil (valued at about $53 million) every year until the completion of the reactors.[55] The Korean Peninsula Energy Development Organization (KEDO) was created in March 1995 to help fund the construction of the reactors, and the nuclear crisis in the Korean Peninsula seemed to have been peacefully resolved.

However, all the Agreed Framework did was to freeze North Korea's nuclear weapons development, halting the further production of weapons-grade plutonium. The agreement made no mention of prior nuclear weapons development, nor did it require North Korea to dismantle its existing nuclear reactors. At the time, for the United States, freezing the North Korean nuclear weapons development was much easier and more practical than dismantling existing reactors. In 1994, Robert Gallucci, former chief U.S. negotiator with North Korea, accurately summarized the nature of the Agreed Framework as having "addressed but not resolved the problem of the known North Korean nuclear weapons program."[56] Consequently, North Korea kept enough weapons-grade plutonium to produce one to two nuclear weapons and 8,000 nuclear fuel rods. At the same time, the United States assessed that, if the Agreed Framework had not been in place, North Korea would have possessed enough weapons-grade plutonium to produce 60–80 nuclear weapons by about 2000 and 40–55 nuclear weapons per year.[57] In effect, the agreement simply postponed the resolution of many of the problems concerning North Korean nuclear weapons development, while the United States took advantage of the ambivalent North Korean nuclear situation to prevent Japan from making any independent diplomatic moves. This ambivalence became a useful tactic for the United States, allowing it to maintain the U.S.-Japan alliance and to station its armed forces in Japan.

Although the United States sent North Korea a clear message that Washington would not tolerate the proliferation of nuclear weapons, in ignoring North Korea's previous development of nuclear weapons, the United States simply maintained the status quo in the Korean Peninsula, transferring substantial financial burden to South Korea and Japan in the process. Indeed, one of the United States' main objectives in the Korean peninsula was to maintain the status quo without war, without unification, without détente, and without too much effort. At the same time, the United States made the best use of North Korea as a surrogate for the Soviet Union in order to devise a pseudo-Cold War environment in East Asia, claiming that East Asia remained unstable and under threat. In doing so, the United States somewhat inflated the North Korean threat and cast North Korea as the "other" in an effort to manage Japan's independent behavior and to keep Japan in the U.S.-Japan alliance.[58] In other words, the continuous existence of North Korea as a plausible threat made it easier for the United States to control Japan's behavior.

China did not remain an aloof bystander, but gradually came to the fore in the mid-1990s. By way of a warning to the Republic of China (ROC) under Lee Teng-hui, the PRC fired a series of missiles in 1995 and 1996. The United States sent two aircraft carriers to patrol the Taiwan Strait. No conflicts broke out, but this crisis provided further evidence of the pseudo-Cold War structure that existed in the Taiwan Strait and demonstrated that the United States was willing to resort to uncompromising measures in the case of such a security emergency in East Asia. These events also helped solidify the U.S.-Japan alliance and Japan's dependence on the United States.

The way in which the U.S.-Japan alliance was to be redefined was spelled out in February 1995, when the U.S. Defense Department released its third East Asia strategy review (the so-called Nye report).[59] The Nye report underscored the importance of security in the Asia-Pacific region and proclaimed that the United States intended to keep a military force of 100,000 troops in the region. It reconfirmed the Japan-U.S. relationship as the necessary foundation for both U.S. security policy in the Asia-Pacific region and U.S. global strategy in general.[60]

In April 1996, President Clinton and Prime Minister Ryutaro Hashimoto signed the "Japan-US Joint Declaration on Security: Alliance for the 21st Century."[61] The declaration stated that "the Asia-Pacific region has become the most dynamic area of the globe." Nevertheless, the declaration also contained the assertion that "instability and uncertainty persist in the region" due to the pseudo-Cold War structure that had prompted the two countries to repeat the by now familiar refrain that a "continued US military presence is also essential for preserving peace and stability in the Asia-Pacific region." Not surprisingly, the new U.S.-Japan guidelines for defense cooperation issued in September 1997 said: "Although the Cold War has ended, the potential for instability and uncertainty persists in the Asia-Pacific region," followed by the usual conclusion: "Accordingly, the maintenance of peace and stability in this region has assumed greater importance for the security of Japan."[62]

By using, and somewhat exaggerating, the North Korean threat and recreating a pseudo-Cold War structure in East Asia, the United States was successful in preventing Japan from extricating itself from the U.S.-Japan alliance. On the other hand, by trying to adopt a more autonomous stance, Japan was successful in keeping U.S. military commitment in East Asia and solidifying the Japan-U.S. alliance.

U.S.-Japan Complementary Relationship

In August 1990, Iraq invaded Kuwait. President George H.W. Bush asked Prime Minister Kaifu for financial assistance, transportation means for a multinational force, and the dispatch of minesweepers or supply ships.[63] Recognizing the constitutional restriction, Washington did not ask Japan to dispatch its Self-Defense Forces (SDF) to participate in the multinational forces, nor did the United States expect Japan to make a substantial military contribution. What the United States needed from Japan was its financial contribution and nominal military assistance in the form of logistical support. Indeed, the U.S. military forces alone were far superior to the Iraqi forces; the United States desired the cooperation of multinational forces in order to gain international legitimacy for its military action in Iraq. Although many countries, including the United States, criticized Japan for resorting to check-book diplomacy or not contributing by way of human resources, Japan did partly what President Bush had expected of it. In the end, Japan contributed $13 billion to the war effort—over one quarter of all war expenditure.[64] During the war, Japan provided the multinational forces with a variety of goods, including four-wheel drive vehicles,[65] and after the war, from April through October 1991, Japan dispatched its minesweepers of the Maritime SDF to the Persian Gulf.

Minesweeping was not enough. Taking international criticism, especially U.S. criticism, to heart, the Japanese government considered it necessary to make a more active military contribution to the United Nations (UN) in terms of human resources. This move was also anticipated by the United States. As Robert O. Keohane argues, the United States expected Japan to provide assistance to refugees and to devise reconstruction plans for troubled regions under the auspices of the UN.[66] In October 1991, Prime Minister Kiichi Miyazawa stated that Japan's contribution "should include some 'sweating' or dispatch of personnel to assist UN peacekeeping operations … [rather than solely depending on] a lavish scattering around of aid."[67] Consequently, in June 1992, Japan enacted the International Peace Cooperation Law (PKO Law). Based on this law, Japan dispatched its SDF five times to participate in the UN Peacekeeping Operations abroad during the 1990s. Japan sent 1,200 SDF personnel to Cambodia in 1992–1993; 144 to Mozambique in 1993–1995; 118 to Zaire (now, the Democratic Republic of Congo) in 1994; 1,463 to Golan Heights in 1996–2013; and 113 to Indonesia in 1999–2000. Japan also dispatched its SDF to Rwanda and East Timor in the 1990s in order to participate in refugee relief activities.[68] Japan's efforts contributed to bringing and maintaining stability in these volatile areas, thereby supplementing the United States' post-Cold War strategic goals.

Throughout the 1990s, Japan also used its Official Development Assistance (ODA) as a political tool, supplementing the United States' post-Cold

War strategic goals. This again was indicative of the implicit division of labor between the United States and Japan; the United States was primarily responsible for the military and strategic aspects, while Japan was responsible for the economic aspect of managing the post-Cold War international order. By 1991, Japan's ODA surpassed $10 billion, making it the largest aid donor in the world. Japan created its ODA charter in 1992, which gave primary consideration to the political conditions for receiving ODA—whether the recipients were linked to the development of weapons of mass destruction and whether they were serious about fostering democracy. [69]

In the 1990s, Washington envisioned this kind of division of labor or complementary relationship between the United States and Japan; in effect, the United States would establish the general framework of strategic initiatives, and Japan, as a junior partner of the United States, would make these initiatives a practical reality by contributing financially, endorsing and legitimizing U.S. initiatives, and making military contributions as broadly as possible. This complementary relationship was an effective way for the United States to realize its strategic goals and to keep Japan in the U.S.-Japan alliance. During the Cold War, the United States as a hegemonic power provided Japan with the military shield and economic benefits, while in the post-Cold War era, the United States was Japan's senior partner, but Japan came to play a more important and complementary role to U.S. leadership, which satisfied Japan's self-esteem and national pride.

The United States' Implicit Prejudiced View of Japan

Under the Agreed Framework, the United States unilaterally promised North Korea to create the KEDO and to finance the construction of a new civilian nuclear reactor, along with other KEDO operations. Yet, in doing so, it passed the financial responsibilities to South Korea and Japan. The United States implicitly believed that its own interest would naturally be shared by Japan. In other words, if Washington felt it was necessary, it could make decisions that would affect Japan without meaningful consultation with Tokyo.

In November 1998, under pressure from the United States, Japan reluctantly agreed to provide KEDO with $1 billion, and South Korea allocated $3.2 billion to fund the construction of the reactor, which was estimated at $4.6 billion. In effect, South Korea and Japan agreed to cover more than 90 percent of KEDO's costs. Because of opposition from the U.S. Congress, the United States only promised to provide North Korea with 500,000 tons of heavy fuel oil per year, valued at about $53 million. [70] Under the circumstances, Japan could not fail to observe that the United States had gone over its head to negotiate unilaterally with North Korea about issues having a direct bearing on Japan's national security. This U.S. attitude may be described as a demonstration of the United States' condescending view of Japan. American leaders placed themselves above Japan and believed that they could make appropriate decisions on the behalf of Japan.

Another example of this implicit prejudice may be found in the Nye report. As this report stated, "Security is like oxygen: you do not tend to notice it until you begin to lose it." With respect to the forward deployment of U.S. forces, the report said: "The American security presence has helped provide this 'oxygen' for East Asian development."[71] In other words, the embedded assumption was that growth in East Asia had only become possible because of the U.S. contribution to the region that had previously been devoid of this vital life-supporting ingredient. In the minds of U.S. policymakers, the region would quickly plunge into chaos if America were to disengage. Such thinking made any earlier Cold War-related justifications for the U.S. presence in East Asia irrelevant and vividly illustrated the condescending view of East Asia held at the top levels of U.S. government.[72] As long as this prejudiced view prevailed, it was next to impossible for the United States to allow Japan to take complete and independent control over its diplomatic and security policies. In light of this, it was an inevitable choice for the United States to maintain the U.S.-Japan alliance in order to contain Japan's independent moves.

In sum, in the post-Cold War era, the United States' efforts to build a pseudo-Cold War structure in East Asia and to establish a complementary relationship between the United States and Japan, along with its implicit prejudiced view of Japan and Asia in general, maintained and strengthened the U.S.-Japan alliance.

CONCLUDING OBSERVATIONS

My research question addressed why the structural realists' prediction that the U.S.-Japan alliance would inevitably weaken or vanish has not been realized over the two decades since the end of the Cold War. In order to answer this question, this chapter placed Japan's security policy in the post-Cold War period within the long-term context of post-World War II U.S.-Japan security relations. This chapter has verified my working hypothesis that, in the post-Cold War period, the United States succeeded in creating a dynamic in East Asia that was similar to the one created during the Cold War. In other words, the United States modified the U.S.-Japan alliance through three main measures: (a) orchestrating a pseudo-Cold War environment in East Asia, (b) seeking to establish a complementary U.S.-Japan relationship that would satisfy and manage Japan's more active role in the international arena, and (c) enacting measures sparked by the United States' prejudiced view of Japan. These three measures in the post-Cold War period are comparable to the three factors during the Cold War: (a) fear of the communist threat, (b) the United States as a hegemonic power, and (c) the United States' prejudiced view of Japan. Because of this development, both the United States and Japan have found it rational and beneficial to maintain the U.S.-Japan alliance even in the post-Cold War period.

NOTES

1. Kenneth N. Waltz, "The Emerging Structure of International Politics," *International Security* 18, no. 2 (1993), pp. 44–79; Kenneth Waltz, "Structural Realism After the Cold War," *International Security* 25, no. 1 (2000), pp. 5–41.

2. George Friedman and Meredith LeBard, *The Coming War with Japan* (New York: St. Martin's, 1991).

3. Robert A. Fisher, "The Erosion of Japanese Pacifism: The Constitutionality of the 1997 U.S.-Japan Defense Guidelines," *Cornell International Law Journal* 32, no. 2 (1999), pp. 393–430; Go Ito, "Redefining Security Roles: Japan's Response to the September 11 Terrorism," *Journal of East Asian Studies* 2, no. 1 (2002), pp. 285–305; Michael J. Green, *Japan's Reluctant Realism: Foreign Policy Challenges in an Era of Uncertain Power* (New York: Palgrave Macmillan, 2003); Christopher W. Hughes, "Japan's Re-Emergence as a 'Normal' Military Power," *Adelphi Papers* pp. 368–69 (London: International Institute for Strategic Studies, 2004); Kamiya Matake, "Naze Jieitai wo Iraku ni Haken surunoka" [Why do we dispatch the Self-Defense Forces to Iraq?], *Gaiko Forum* 187 (2004), pp. 24–28; Satoshi Morimoto, *Iraku Senso to Jieitai Haken* [The Iraq War and Dispatching Japan's Self-Defense Forces] (Tokyo: Toyo Keizai Shimposha, 2004); Tomohito Shinoda, *Kantei Gaiko* [The Prime Minister's Official Residence Diplomacy] (Tokyo: Asahi Shimbunsha, 2004); Kyoko Hatakeyama, "Japan's Changed Perceptions Towards Security Issues," *CJES Research Papers* 2005, no. 3 (2005); Masayuki Tadokoro, "Change and Continuity in Japan's 'Abnormalcy': An Emerging External Attitude of the Japanese Public," in *Japan As a 'Normal Country'?* eds. Yoshihide Soeya, Masayuki Tadokoro, and David A. Welch (Toronto: University of Toronto Press, 2011); Yongwook Ryu, "The Road to Japan's 'Normalization': Japan's Foreign Policy Orientation since the 1990s," *Korean Journal of Defense Analysis* 19, no. 2 (2007), pp. 63–88.

4. Stephen M. Walt, "Keeping the World 'Off-Balance': Self-Restraint and U.S. Foreign Policy," in *America Unrivaled the Future of the Balance of Power* ed. by G. John Ikenberry (Ithaca and London: Cornell University Press, 2002), pp. 121-54.

5. Stephen M. Walt, *The Origins of Alliances* (Ithaca, NY: Cornell University Press, 1990), p. 25.

6. Susanne Klien, *Rethinking Japan's Identity and International Role: Tradition and Change in Japan's Foreign Policy* (London: Routledge, 2002).

7. David Arase, "Japan, the Active State? Security Policy after 9/11," *Asian Survey* 47, no. 4 (2007), pp. 560–83.

8. William C. Wohlforth, "The Stability of a Unipolar World," in *America's Strategic Choices*, ed. Michael E. Brown et al., revised edition (Cambridge, MA: MIT Press, 2000); William C. Wohlforth, "U.S. Strategy in a Unipolar World," in *America Unrivaled*, pp. 98–118.

9. Thomas Risse, "U.S. Power in a Liberal Security Community," in *America Unrivaled,* pp. 260–83.

10. Takafumi Ohtomo, "Bandwagoning to Dampen Suspicion: NATO and the US-Japan Alliance After the Cold War," *International Relations of the Asia-Pacific* 3 (2003), pp. 29–55.

11. Paul Midford, "The Logic of Reassurance and Japan's Grand Strategy," *Security Studies* 11, no. 3 (2002), pp. 1–43.

12. Jennifer M. Lind, "Pacifism or Passing the Buck? Testing Theories of Japanese Security Policy," *International Security* 29, no. 1 (2004), pp. 92–121.

13. Peter J. Katzenstein and Nobuo Okawara, "Japan's National Security: Structures, Norms, and Policies," *International Security* 17, no. 4 (1993), pp. 84–118; Thomas U. Berger, "From Sword to Chrysanthemum: Japan's Culture of Anti-militarism," *International Security* 17, no. 4 (1993), pp. 119–50; Peter J. Katzenstein and Nobuo Okawara, *Japan's National Security: Structures, Norms, and Policy Responses in a Changing World* (Ithaca, NY: East Asia Program, Cornell University, 1993); Peter J. Katzenstein, *Cultural Norms and National Security: Police and Military in Postwar Japan* (Ithaca, NY: Cornell University Press, 1996); Glenn D. Hook, *Militarization and Demilitarization in Contemporary Japan* (London: Routledge, 1996); Thomas U. Berger, *Cultures of Antimilitarism: National Security in Germany and Japan* (Baltimore, MD: Johns Hopkins University Press, 1998); and Thomas U. Berger, "The Pragmatic Liberalism of an Adaptive State," in *Japan in International Politics the Foreign Policies of an Adaptive State*, eds. Thomas U. Berger, Mike M. Mochizuki, and Jitsuo Tsuchiyama (Boulder, CO: Lynne Rienner, 2007), pp. 259–99.

14. Yoshihide Soeya, "A 'Normal' Middle Power: Interpreting Changes in Japanese Security Policy in the 1990s and After," in *Japan As a 'Normal Country'?*, pp. 72–97.

15. Kenneth B. Pyle, *Japan Rising: The Resurgence of Japanese Power and Purpose* (New York: Public Affairs, 2007).

16. Takeshi Watanabe, *Senryoka no Nihon Zaisei Oboegaki* [Memorandum of Japan's Finance under the Occupation] (Tokyo: Nihon Keizai Shimbunsha, 1966), p. 291.

17. Yonosuke Nagai and Akira Iriye eds., *The Origins of the Cold War in Asia* (New York: Columbia University Press, 1977); John Lewis Gaddis, *The United States and the Origins of the Cold War, 1941-1947* (New York: Columbia University Press, 1972).

18. Yoneyuki Sugita, *Hegemoni no Gyakusetsu – Ajia Taiheiyo Senso to Beikoku no Higashi Ajia Seisaku, 1941nen – 1952nen* [Paradox of Hegemony – Asia-Pacific War and U.S. Policies toward East Asia, 1941-1952] (Kyoto: Sekai Shisosha, 1999).

19. Thomas McCormick, *America's Half-Century: United States Foreign Policy in the Cold War* (Baltimore: The Johns Hopkins University Press, 1989), p. 5.

20. Memorandum by Charles Spinks, 29 September 1951, *Records of the U.S. Department of State Relating to United States Political Relations with Japan* (hereafter, *USPR*) *1950-1954* (Wilmington, DE: Scholarly Resources, 1987)，Reel #1.

21. G. C. Allen, *Japan's Economic Recovery* (London: Oxford University Press, 1958), p. 33; Catherine Edwards, "US Policy Towards Japan, 1945-1951: Rejection of Revolution," (Ph.D. dissertation, University of California, Los Angeles, 1977), p. 163.

22. Aaron Forsberg, *America and the Japanese Miracle* (Chapel Hill, NC: The University of North Carolina Press, 2000).

23. Central Intelligence Agency (CIA), NIE-52，29 May 1952，President's Secretary's File, *Papers of Harry S Truman* [hereafter *PHST*].

24. Office of Intelligence Research, the Department of State, 27 December 1951, *Records of the U.S. Department of State Relating to the Internal Affairs of Japan 1950-1954* (Wilmington, DE: Scholarly Resources, 1987), Reel #1.

25. Trade Statistics," Ministry of Finance, http://www.customs.go.jp/toukei/suii/html/nenbet.htm.

26. YoshioAsai, "1950nendai Zenhan niokeru Gaishi Donyu Mondai (Jo)" [Introduction of Foreign Capital in the First Half of the 1950s (I)], *Seijo Daigaku Keizai Kenkyu* 153 (2001).

27. http://shouwashi.com/transition-trade_balance.html

28. Forsberg, *America and the Japanese Miracle*.

29. Sayuri Shimizu, *Creating People of Plenty: The United States and Japan's Economic Alternatives, 1950-1960* (Kent, OH: The Kent State University Press, 2001).

30. Ping He, "Nihon no Gaishi Donyu ni Kansuru Kosatsu: 1960nen – 1973nen" [A Note on Foreign Capital Policy in Japan : 1960-1973], *Yokohama Kokusai Shakai Kagaku Kenkyu* 13, no. 6 (2009), pp. 12–14.

31. Forsberg, *America and the Japanese Miracle*.

32. Ken Togo, "Betonamu Senso to Higashi Ajia no Keizai Seicho" [Vietnam War and East Asian Economic Growth], *Musashi University Working Paper* 18 (J-10) (2013); Sohyo Chosabu [Research Department of the General Council of Trade Unions of Japan], "Betonamu

Tokuju to Nihon Keizai" [Vietnam War Special Procurements and Japanese Economy], *Sohyo Chosa Geppo* 2 (November 1966).

33. Louis Hartz, *The Liberal Tradition in America* (San Diego: Horcourt, Brace and Company, 1955); Saito Makoto, *Amerika no Bunmyaku* [Context of the United States] (Tokyo: Iwanami Shoten, 1981); Gordon S. Wood, *The Creation of the American Republic 1776-1787* (New York: W. W. Norton & Company, 1969).

34. Futoshi Shibayama, *Nihon Saigunbi eno Michi-1945-1954nen* [Toward Japan's Rearmament, 1945-1954] (Kyoto: Minerva Shobo, 2010), p. 63.

35. CIA, 25 July 1949, Intelligence Memorandum No. 197, Records of the National Security Council, *PHST*.

36. Memorandum by Charles Spinks, 29 September 1951, *USPR 1950-1954*, Reel #1.

37. Nakanishi Hiroshi, "Yoshida/Daresu Kaidan Saiko" [Review of the Yoshida–Dulles Meetings], *Hogaku Ronso* 140, no. 1/2 (1996), p. 224.

38. Dulles to Nitze, 20 July 1950, United States Department of State, *Foreign Relations of the United States*, Vol. VI, East Asia and the Pacific (Washington, DC: U.S. Government Printing Office, 1950), p. 1247.

39. *Asahi Shimbun*, 19 August 1950, in Ohtake Hideo, *Sengo Nihon Boei Mondai Shiryoshu* [Documents of Postwar Japanese Defense Issues], Vol. 1 (Tokyo: Sanichi Shobo, 1991), p. 430.

40. John Lewis Gaddis, *The Long Peace: Inquiries into the History of the Cold War* (New York: Oxford University Press, 1987).

41. Yoneyuki Sugita, "Reisengo no Anzen Hosho" [National Security after the Cold War], *Igzamina* (June 1996).

42. John Dower, "The San Francisco System: Past, present, future in United States-Japan-China relations," in Kimie Hara ed., *The San Francisco System and Its Legacies* (London: Routledge, 2015), p. 221.

43. Yasuhiro Maeda, "Chosen Hanto no 'Kaku' wo meguru Shomondai" [Various Problems on 'Nuclear' on the Korean Peninsula], in *Chosen Hanto no Hikakuka to Nihon* [Denuclearization on the Korean Peninsula and Japan], ed. Kan Keigyoku (Osaka: Keizai Hoka Daigaku Shuppanbu, 1995), p. 67.

44. Ibid., p. 67.

45. Mark E. Caprio, "Kurinton Seiken ka no Beicho Gaiko Kankei – Funso to Ketsudan no Kikan-" [U.S.-North Korean Diplomatic Relationship under the Clinton Administration –Period of Conflicts and Decisios-], in *Kita Chosen to Tohoku Ajia no Kokusai Shin Chitsujo* [North Korea and International New Order in Northeast Asia], ed. Hideo Kobayashi (Tokyo: Gakubunsha, 2001), pp. 95–96.

46. John Feffer, "U.S.-North Korea Relations," *Foreign Policy in Focus* 4, no. 15 (1999), p. 1.

47. Yoneyuki Sugita, "A Never-Ending Story: Inflating the Threat from North Korea," *The Journal of Pacific Asia* Vol. 11 (2004).

48. David Albright, "Prologue," in *Solving the North Korean Nuclear Puzzle*, eds. David Albright and Kevin O'Neill (Washington, DC: Institute for Science and International Security Press), pp. 7-8.

49. Former President William Clinton confirmed this military attack plan in his lecture at Rotterdam, the Netherlands on 15 December 2002. *Yomiuri Shimbun* 17 December 2002.

50. David C. Kang and Victor D. Cha, "Think Again: The Korea Crisis," *Foreign Policy* 136 (2003).

51. Report of the Advisory Group on Defense Issues, "The Modality of Security and Defense Capability of Japan: The Outlook for the 21st Century" (Higuchi Report), 12 August 1994. http://www.ioc.u-tokyo.ac.jp/~worldjpn/documents/texts/JPSC/19940812.O1E.html

52. Report of the Advisory Group on Defense Issues, "The Modality of Security and Defense Capability of Japan: The Outlook for the 21st Century" (Higuchi Report) http://www.ioc.u-tokyo.ac.jp/~worldjpn/documents/texts/JPSC/19940812.O1E.html

53. Sugita, "A Never-Ending Story."

54. "Agreed Framework between the United States of America and the Democratic People's Republic of Korea," Geneva, 21 October 1994. http://www.iaea.org/Publications/Documents/Infcircs/Others/infcirc457.pdf

55. Robert L. Gallucci, "The U.S.-DPRK Agreed Framework," House International Relations Committee Subcommittee on Asia and the Pacific, 23 February 1995.

56. "Progress and Challenges in Denuclearizing North Korea," *Arms Control Today*, May 2002.

57. Albright, "Prologue," p. 11.

58. Christopher W. Hughes argues that the perceived threat of North Korea did influence Japan's security policies. See, Christopher W. Hughes, "'Super-Sizing' the DPRK Threat: Japan's Evolving Military Posture and North Korea," *Asian Survey* 49, no. 2 (March/April 2009).

59. Office of International Security Affairs, Department of Defense, "United States Security Strategy for the East Asia-Pacific Region," 27 February 1995. http://www.ioc.u-tokyo.ac.jp/~worldjpn/documents/texts/JPUS/19950227.O1E.html

60. As for American values demonstrated in the Nye report, see Yoneyuki Sugita, "Dai Sanji Higashi Ajia Senryaku Hokokusho (the Nye report) ni Mirareru Amerikateki Kachikan" [American values demonstrated in the third East Asia strategy review (the Nye report)], in *Amerikateki Kachikan no Yuragi* [Fluctuation of American Values] (Tokyo: Sanwa Shoseki, 2006), pp. 1–7.

61. "Japan-US Joint Declaration on Security: Alliance for the 21st Century" (17 April 1996) http://www.mofa.go.jp/region/n-america/us/security/security.html

62. Ministry of Foreign Affairs of Japan, "Joint Statement U.S.-Japan Security Consultative Committee Completion of the Review of the Guidelines for U.S.-Japan Defense Cooperation New York, New York," 23 September 1997. http://www.mofa.go.jp/region/n-america/us/security/defense.html

63. Seisaku Kenkyu Daigakuin Daigaku C.O.E. Oralu/Seisaku Kenkyu Project, *Kuriyama Takakazu (Moto Chubei Taishi) Oralu Hisutori – Wangan Senso to Nihon Gaiko* [Oral History of Kuriyama Takakazu (Former Japanese ambassador to the United States) – the Gulf War and Japanese Diplomacy] (Tokyo: Seisaku Kenkyu Daigakuin Daigaku, 2005), p. 39.

64. Kan Keigyoku, "Amerika no Shin Senryaku to Chosen Hanto no Hikakuka" [America's New Strategy and Denuclearization of the Korean Peninsula], in *Chosen Hanto no Hikakuka to Nihon*, ed. Kan Keigyoku (Osaka: Osaka keizai hoka daigaku shuppanbu, 1995), p. 11.

65. Nakanishi Hiroshi, "Wangan Senso to Nihon Gaiko," [The Gulf War and Japanese Diplomacy] Nippon.com (6 December 2011) http://www.nippon.com/ja/features/c00202/

66. Robert O. Keohane, "Nihon wa Oubun no Ridashippu wo" [Japan Should Assume Appropriate Leadership!], *Ekonomisuto*, 8 April 1991.

67. *Mainichi Daily News* (Tokyo), 20 October 1991.

68. Ministry of Defense http://www.mod.go.jp/j/approach/kokusai_heiwa/list.html and http://www.mod.go.jp/j/approach/kokusai_heiwa/katudou/2007.html.

69. Julie Gilson, "Building Peace or Following the Leader? Japan's Peace Consolidation Diplomacy," *Pacific Affairs* 80, no. 1 (2007), p. 36.

70. Richard P Cronin, "Averting trouble in China and North Korea," *The Fletcher Forum of World Affairs* (Winter, 2005), p. 4.

71. "United States Security Strategy for the East Asia-Pacific Region,"(27 February 1995) http://www.ioc.u-tokyo.ac.jp/~worldjpn/documents/texts/JPUS/19950227.O1E.html

72. Sugita, "Dai Sanji Higashi Ajia Senryaku Hokokusho pp. 1-7.

Chapter Two

Experiences of Japanese American Soldiers in the Korean War

Analyzing the Case of a
Nisei *Woman's Military Service and Resettlement*

Miyuki Daimaruya, Project Research Fellow,
Ochanomizu University

This chapter[1] analyzes the service experiences of Japanese Americans[2] in the Korean War (1950-1953). Particularly, the study focuses on the cases of Californian *Nisei* (second-generation Japanese immigrants). Compared with the recent popularity and reputations within U.S. society for racially segregated units who fought during World War II, such as the United States Army 442nd Regimental Combat Team and the 100th Infantry Battalion, the presence of *Nisei* soldiers in the Korean War has been undervalued in American history for a long time. However, the history of *Nisei* soldiers in the Korean War is important for re-considering the lives of Japanese Americans on the West Coast of the U.S. following their wartime imprisonment in Japanese American internment camps.[3]

This chapter will investigate the impact of military service during the Korean War on the postwar lives of *Nisei*. More specifically, the chapter examines, through the individual case of a *Nisei* veteran, how Korean War military service by *Nisei* affected their *resettlement* processes after they left the camps. For Japanese Americans, the Korean War period was also their *resettlement-era*. The *resettlement* is a term widely used both in daily life among Japanese Americans and at the academic level to describe the process of social reintegration of Japanese Americans or the reconstruction of their ordinary lives after leaving the internment camps.[4]

The term *resettlement* as it applied to Japanese Americans requires a detailed definition. The *resettlement* contains two different meanings: One is the *resettlement* policy of the War Relocation Authority (WRA) during World War II; the other is the mobilization of Japanese American internees who returned to their homes on the West Coast after January 1945, following the December 1944 United States Supreme Court decision in *Ex parte Endo*, which ruled that the WRA could no longer imprison Japanese Americans and must release them from the camps. In this chapter, I describe the former as "wartime *resettlement*" and the latter as "post-internment *resettlement*." Most previous studies of the immediate post-war experience of Japanese Americans define the period of the *resettlement* as running from around June 1942 to June 1952.[5]

Herein, the analysis of the military service of *Nisei* in the Korean War during the *resettlement* mainly focuses on the case of a woman veteran, Kiyo Sato, who was born in Sacramento, California, in 1923 and served in the United States Air Force Nurse Corps (AFNC) during the Korean War. Most *Nisei* soldiers who served in the Korean War were men; however, a few women soldiers, such as Sato, volunteered.

The chapter investigates her autobiography, *Kiyo's Story: A Japanese American Family's Quest for the American Dream* (2009),[6] and my interviews with her. My interviews with Sato were conducted twice in Sacramento, at my temporary accommodation and at her home. The first interview was on November 17, 2010 and the second was on March 24, 2011. The interviews adopted a semi-structured style.[7] I also corresponded with her by e-mail, telephone, and letters, which provided me with a rich set of communications that further informed my understanding of her experiences of the past. The chapter also uses several other sources, such as the autobiography of a *Nisei* Korean War male veteran,[8] interviews with several male veterans, and newspaper articles, in order to construct a more comprehensive version of the *forgotten* history of *Nisei* soldiers in the Korean War.

Through analyzing the personal experiences of Sato, the chapter reveals how *Nisei* military service in the Korean War affected her post-World War II *resettlement* process as a *Nisei* woman. In Sato's case, her status as a U.S. citizen drastically transformed after her service in the Korean War, as this service facilitated her social involvement after her internment experience.

The chapter is divided into four parts. The first and the second parts provide general information about *Nisei* soldiers serving during the Korean War and their service backgrounds, in order to aid in understanding Sato's personal experience as a *Nisei* woman in the U.S. military during the early Cold War. The first part investigates the impact on their lives of *Nisei's* military services in the Korean War. It examines how their experiences of internment were a backdrop and motivation for serving in the military during the time of the Korean War.

The second part investigates the social impact *of Nisei's* service in the Korean War. It discusses social roles of *Nisei* soldiers in the U.S. of the 1950s. Today, the presence of *Nisei* soldiers in the Korean War is largely forgotten; however, the U.S. government in the 1950s encouraged *Nisei* service in the Korean War because the presence of *Nisei* soldiers could represent the military service of model *ethnic minorities* under the early Cold War system. The U.S. government used images of *Nisei* serving in racially-integrated units to demonstrate that the U.S. was achieveing a racially equal society in the period.

The third and fourth parts analyze the case of Sato. They investigate how Sato's military service affected her *resettlement* process as a *Nisei* woman and also examine how gender differences affected her personal experience as a *Nisei* soldier. So, the third part discusses Sato's process of *resettlement* following her whole life as a *Nisei* woman. This part tries to understand her *resettlement* process using *home* theory, which is derived from geographical studies.

The fourth part reconsiders Sato's military service during the early Cold War era, examining how Sato's service experiences reflected U.S. politics of the 1950s with respect to both gender and ethnicity. More specifically, the part highlights why she could serve in the AFNC even though she was a *Nisei* woman in a subjugated status in U.S. society at that time.

LEGACY OF WORLD WAR II INTERNMENT AND POSTWAR *RESETTLEMENT*

First, who was the *Nisei* soldier in the Korean War? The most salient feature of *Nisei* soldiers in the Korean War is that they were placed in racially integrated units. Most of these service people were *Nisei* men. The official number of *Nisei* who served during the Korean War is unknown, but both the United States Department of Defense (DOD) and the Korean War Japanese American Veterans Association suggest that 5,000–6,000 *Nisei* men were on active duty during the Korean War period, with 2,000–3,000 dispatched to the Korean Peninsula as combat soldiers.[9] Some *Nisei* women also volunteered for duty in regular military units during the Korean War, but most completed their service without leaving the U.S., or were stationed in U.S. bases all over the world, as in Sato's case. The number of *Nisei* causalities in Korea is unclear. However, the Korean War Japanese Americans Veterans Association in California has found 256 Korean battlefield Japanese American casualties.[10] This veterans' group predicts more casualties of Japanese ancestry will be discovered.[11]

Then, how did the military service of *Nisei* in the Korean War affect their lives as *Nisei* after their internment during World War II, and what was the historical background of their service? The history of *Nisei* soldiers in the Korean War has scarcely been evaluated in the U.S. Even today, there are few studies about the military service of *Nisei* after dissolving the 442nd in June 1946. The previous studies of both Edwin Nakasone and Yukiko Yanagida discuss the presence of *Nisei* in the military during the Korean War; however, their arguments are mainly focused on *Nisei*'s service during World War II.[12] These studies focus only on particular veterans who had fighting experiences in both World War II and the Korean War. Mainly, these studies focus on the story of *Nisei* in the 442nd, with service experience during the Korean War just treated as "the second war" for the former-442nd. The presence of *Nisei* soldiers in the Korean War is thus hidden behind the declarative and tragic history of the 442nd. However, the military service of *Nisei* during the Korean War was also a legacy of the internment and experiences of Japanese Americans during the former decade. *Nisei* soldiers in the Korean War in the early 1950s, served in the military in order to pursue better lives after their hardest time of internment in the 1940s.

The history of Japanese Americans in the 1940s requires some discussion in order to understand the position of this group in American society during the 1950s, particularly as they tried to resume their lives post-World War II in the U.S. Why has the military history of *Nisei* only focused on the 442nd Regimental combat team and the 100th Infantry battalion during World War II? One possible answer is that the concentration of World War II-period studies was a result of the particular events of Japanese Americans in the 1940s—evacuation from their homes and then wartime internment camps on the West Coast of the mainland. The trauma and tragic injustice of these events dominated the history of Japanese American experience during World War II for subsequent decades.

By 1940, there were about 130,000 Japanese Americans living on the West Coast. The state of California held the most significant population of Japanese Americans in the mainland U.S. In March 1942, several months after Japan's imperial navy attacked Pearl Harbor on December 7, 1941, initiating the U.S.-Japan Pacific War, U.S. President Franklin D. Roosevelt signed Executive Order 9066, which authorized the removal of Japanese Americans living on the West Coast to internment camps. By May 1942, the U.S. government had moved all Japanese Americans from the West Coast, a total of 127,000 people.[13] All internment camps were closed in 1946. When the U.S.-Japan Pacific War began, the draft and registration of *Nisei* men were prohibited. After implementing "loyalty registration" by the WRA in camps, military recruitment of *Nisei* restarted in February 1943.[14] The purpose of this registration for all internees who were over seventeen years old, both *Issei* (native-born Japanese who emigrated to the U.S.) and *Nisei,* was to specify their loyalty for the U.S. and recant any allegiance to the Japanese Emperor.

The unique and shocking situation of all Japanese Americans in the West Coast during the Pacific War is one apparent cause for the concentration of social interest in *Nisei* soldiers only during the World War II period. In fact, the 442nd, the World War II *Nisei* segregated unit, is now known to have suffered the worst rate of casualties in U.S. army history. The huge sacrifices of segregated *Nisei* units during World War II are now considered valiant demonstrations of bravery and loyalty to the U.S. by Japanese Americans. The historian Takashi Fujitani has explained the special attention U.S. society has given *Nisei* units during World War II:

> To be sure, not all [but many] who live in the United States today have heard about the military exploits of the 100th Infantry Battalion or the 442nd Regimental Combat Team, the two segregated units whose members—nearly all Japanese American—were, as the legend goes, the most highly decorated group of soldiers in U.S. history. [15]

In contrast, *Nisei* soldiers who served in the U.S. military during the Korean War have not received any evaluation from the U.S. society.

However, my investigation of *Nisei* military service during the Korean War, whether drafted or volunteered, was valuable in order to understand *Nisei* life and social status in the early days of the Cold War. *Nisei* military service during the Korean War was directly connected to the *resettlement* process of Japanese Americans.

How have previous studies concerning the *resettlement* of Japanese Americans treated the military experience of *Nisei*? For the most part, they have not. [16] Even today, despite a rich variety of sources and perspectives pertaining to the *resettlement* of Japanese Americans, the subject of military service during the *resettlement* remains invisible. However, military service was an immediate issue because the U.S. Army drafted male citizens during the Korea War period. In a study concerning U.S. soldiers during the Korean War, Andrew Huebner notes that from the Korean War era to the late 1950s, "roughly seventy percent of all draft-aged males served in the military. By 1954 there were more living veterans in the United States, some twenty million, than ever before in American history." [17] For *Nisei* draft-age men, military service was as much a duty as it was for any other U.S. male.

Five years passed from the end of the Pacific War and internment until the start of the Korean War in June 1950. During this time, Japan had been converted into a friendly ally of the U.S., and Japanese American citizens were no longer treated as "enemy aliens" by the U.S. government. However, Japanese Americans still faced serious racial discrimination in U.S. society. For *Nisei*, the post-World War II era was still a difficult period, characterized by low social status and the need to obey U.S. governmental policy the same as other ethnic Americans.

Then why did *Nisei* serve in the Korean War, even though their social standing was hardly secure? During my interviews with *Nisei* veterans of the Korean War (including Sato), both volunteers and draftees, most said they were motivated to serve in the military for economic reasons rather than from a desire to show loyalty as U.S. citizens. They served to better their lives or simply trying to conquer racial discrimination against Japanese Americans in U.S. society. For example, a veteran who volunteered for the U.S. Army[18] said exactly this, that he volunteered because he wanted to improve his life as a *Nisei* and to break the racial discrimination against him.

Even though all U.S.-born *Nisei* had U.S. citizenship, racial discrimination prevented them from obtaining adequate employment or access to a college education.[19] Another example, a veteran who was a draftee, said that he was already a university student when the Army called him up in 1951, but that he had to obey the draft because it was his duty as a U.S. citizen.[20] Explaining his motivation to serve, he also said "I could not bring shame to my family."[21]

When *Nisei* soldiers could return home safely after their service, the Korean War GI bill promised equal support to all U.S. veterans, making higher education accessible. Several *Nisei* veterans of the Korean War whom I interviewed used their GI benefits to obtain a university education. In this way, these *Nisei* tried to surmount the difficulties of racial discrimination and reintegration into U.S. society. Military service during the Korean War became a pathway for the successful accomplishment of post-internment *resettlement*. In other words, most *Nisei* who came from the West Coast area and served in the Korean War did so to accomplish their *resettlement* during the fifties.

NISEI SERVICE IN THE KOREAN WAR AND U.S. RACIAL POLICY DURING THE EARLY COLD WAR

Next, let us examine the public presence and roles of *Nisei* soldiers in the Korean War during the 1950s. *Nisei* military service during the Korean War was not only affected by the Japanese American community and their *resettlement* process but also influenced American society widely in terms of ethnic inclusion during the early period of the Cold War. Moreover, *Nisei* soldiers serving in Korea were used by the U.S. government as representative examples of racial integration of minority group soldiers during the 1950s. However, the number of Asian Americans serving in the U.S. military during the Korean War was in fact less than one percent of enlisted personnel.[22] The military population of *Nisei* was very few. Why were *Nisei* in the military selected as a symbol of racial integration during the Cold War? One possible reason is that the *Nisei*'s former enemy ancestry was more suitable for representation than any other Asian Americans.

According to Robert Lee in his book *Orientals,* the myth of the model minority of Asian Americans was born in the early 1950s; his analysis assists in understanding why *Nisei* service in the Korean War represented ethnic integration at this time. Lee indicates that "[t]he narrative of Asian ethnic assimilation fit the requirements of Cold War containment perfectly." In the U.S. military, among Asian Americans, whether by design or default, the most effective at demonstrating the loyalty of Asian Americans to the country were *Nisei* participating in international displays of asserted U.S. supremacy in racial matters.

The presence of fully integrated *Nisei* soldiers in the Korean War was favorable for the U.S. government because equal treatment of *Nisei* in the military enabled the U.S. government to claim that racial equality was proceeding in U.S. society and also demonstrated U.S. supremacy in regard to racial matters to other countries. The U.S. government tried to demonstrate to the entire world that the U.S. was superior to the Soviet Union and other eastern bloc countries because U.S. society had supposedly ended racial discrimination. As Jennifer A. Delton has noted, "anti-communism and the Cold War enabled and fulfilled the New Deal's reform agenda,"[23] which included racial equality measures.

The year of 1948, only two years after the deactivation of the 442nd and two years before the Korean War broke out, had become a remarkable year for all *minority* soldiers in the U.S. military when, in June, U.S. President Harry S. Truman signed Executive Order 9981 and the U.S. Congress passed *The Women's Armed Services Integration Act of 1948.*[24] These actions by the U.S. government reorganized U.S. Armed Forces to accelerate the integration of minorities—both men and women of all races—into the military, in accordance with Cold War liberalization policies. Subsequently, the Korean War was the first active duty opportunity after the 1948 reorganization, and was a turning point that accelerated equal treatment for most U.S. ethnic-*minority* soldiers, the same as *Nisei.*

Nisei in the military were affected by this military transformation in 1948 directly, and the social status of all Japanese Americans was transformed in a short time. A main reason for the transformation is that Japan became a friendly ally of the U.S. and became an important element in the U.S. Cold War system. As mentioned earlier, Japanese Americans in the U.S. quickly went from being enemy hostiles to loyal citizens. At the same time, it appears that the status of *Nisei* in the U.S. military reached an equal footing with all other serving soldiers starting at this time. *Nisei* in the military were integrated into multiracial units in the same way that other ethnic people were integrated.[25] Also, prior to World War II and the internment of Japanese Americans, *Nisei* could serve only in the U.S. Army. However, from 1948

Nisei became eligible for service in the U.S. Navy, Air Force, and Marine Corps. In short, the conditions of military service for *Nisei* drastically changed from the late 1940s and continuing into the Korean War.

Lee also mentions how war images of Asian Americans operated in public in the 1950s and helped the U.S. governmental policy of the early Cold War: "Three specters haunted Cold War America in the 1950s: the red menace of communism, the black menace of race mixing, and the white menace of homosexuality." Following his analysis, *Nisei* in the U.S. military performed a kind of triple duty[26] *containing* the menaces of the Cold War era. In other words, it seems that *Nisei* soldiers in the Korean War had the special social role of *Cold War soldier*. This means *Nisei* soldiers in Korea were symbolic representations of both anti-communism and U.S. domestic racial integration. The image of *Nisei* soldiers in Korea as *Cold War soldiers* was the creation not only of the U.S. government policies of the early cold war but also of a liberal desire for racial equality in U.S. society.

Sergeant Hiroshi "Hershy" Miyamura is the most famous example of a *Nisei* who played the role of *Cold War soldier* in public. On October 27, 1953, Sergeant Miyamura, a *Nisei* veteran who had just returned from the Korean Peninsula, was awarded the U.S. Medal of Honor, the highest medal that can be awarded to a U.S. soldier, by President Dwight D. Eisenhower. Miyamura was the first Japanese American and also the only *Nisei* recipient to be given the Medal of Honor during the Korean War.

For Sergeant Miyamura, the Korean War was his second tour of wartime duty. He was also a veteran of the 442nd during World War II. After he returned from combat in Europe and the Pacific, he decided to remain in the Army, resulting in dispatch to a combat zone on the Korean Peninsula. During heavy fighting he was captured by North Korean troops and spent twenty-eight months in the communist camp. He became a POW.

According to the *New York Times* the day after the Medal of Honor award ceremony at the White House, Sergeant Miyamura and six other veterans received medals and had their photos taken with President Eisenhower.[27] Based on their faces in the photos and family names of veterans, Sergeant Miyamura was the only Asian and the only *ethnic-minority* soldier to be honored that day.

Why was Miyamura selected as a Medal of Honor recipient? Even though Sergeant Miyamura was one of the few miraculous survivors of the 442nd and a career military veteran, he only managed to achieve the rank of sergeant. Miyamura was selected as a recipient and the Government thought him a suitable representative of loyal *Nisei* soldiers for two reasons. First, as an honorable former-442nd, broadcasting Sergeant Miyamura's award all over the country made it easy for the American people to see that the Japanese American, once *the enemy alien*, had now become the representative model *minority* soldier of the U.S. military. Second, the U.S. was consumed by the Red Scare, and returning veterans, especially former POWs, were suspected of having been brainwashed. The American people were especially shocked when twenty-one American soldiers refused to return to the U.S.[28] Miyamura spent twenty-one months in a communist POW camp, and he returned to his own country without hesitation. The presence of Miyamura showed the U.S. *minority* veteran's unshakable loyalty for the U.S.

Not only could the U.S. government use images of *Nisei* soldiers in the Korean War to highlight the acceleration of racial integration of minorities in American society, the images could also be used to mask the oppression of African Americans in the military. As Lee mentions regarding the presence of Asian Americans, "On the home front, it sent a message to 'Negroes and other minorities' that accommodation would be rewarded while militancy would be contained and crushed."

At this time, the U.S. government feared unrest and the growing political activism of African Americans in American public life, as well as in the military. African Americans, who made up seven percent of military personnel, were the largest minority group in the military. I speculate that the U.S. government used *Nisei* soldiers to prevent the advancement of African Americans in the military.

Thus, efforts to promote the social inclusion of Japanese Americans in U.S. society during the 1950s were influenced by the nascent civil rights movement in the African American community and a part of furtive oppression from the government. Lee indicated that Asian Americans were *welcomed* because they were "not black." Lee insists that "the elevation of Asian Americans to the position of model minority had less to do with the actual success of Asian Americans than to the perceived failure—or worse, refusal—of Asian Americans to assimilate. Asian Americans were 'not black' in two significant ways: They were both politically silent and ethnically assailable."[29] *Nisei* soldiers were not only symbols of an asserted racial harmony within the U.S. military, but were also treated as "the ethnic minority who welcomed assimilation,"[30] while other *minorities* were excluded.

Moreover, Japanese American judicial and legal conditions gradually improved during the Cold War. For example, the Immigrant Nationality Act of 1952 was crucial to Japanese American post-internment *resettlement* because this law approved the naturalization of *Issei* living in the U.S. However, while this act provided *Issei* with legalized naturalization, it did nothing to liberalize immigration policy. The main purpose of the Act was to *contain* the Reds and shut out new immigrants to the U.S. considered potential communist spies. Ironically, therefore, the beginning of the Cold War saw the creation of political and legal conditions that helped former Japanese American internees re-enter American society both ideologically and practically.

So why, in contrast to the relatively well-known participation of *Nisei* in World War II, has the presence of *Nisei* in the Korean War, celebrated multiple times in the 1950s, now been forgotten in U.S. society? One reason is that the Korean War did not provide the U.S. with a definitive military victory. In the end, the Korean War was a stalemate, and the presence of *Nisei* soldiers did little to demonstrate U.S. supremacy over the Soviet Union or China. Despite significant changes in U.S. cultural attitudes toward and legal treatment of Asian Americans, symbolized most strongly by *Nisei* soldiers in Korea, they have become, along with a forgotten war, *forgotten soldiers*.

RESETTLEMENT OF AND VOLUNTEERING IN THE AIR FORCE OF A *NISEI* WOMAN SOLDIER

Personal Backgrounds, *Settlement* and Theoretical *Home*

Now, I will focus on a case study of a woman *Nisei* soldier, the previously mentioned Kiyo Sato. Sato is a rare *Nisei* woman soldier. However, investigating her personal experiences of the *resettlement* and her military service in the Korean War also shows us how racial and gender policies in the Cold War U.S. operated and harmonized for her. Part three and part four will discuss how Sato's military service in the Korean War facilitated her re-entry into American society as a *Nisei* woman after her period of World War II internment. I examine how Sato's attempt at *resettlement* led her to volunteer for duty in the U.S. Air Force during the Korean War. Sato's case shows us how the experience of military service was directly connected to the process of her *resettlement*. Also, Sato's case indicates how gender differences affected the lives and experiences of *Nisei* soldiers. Part three investigates the *resettlement* process that led Sato to volunteer in the Air Force during the Korean War.

Let us review Sato's personal background in detail and review her *resettlement* process from World War II to the Korean War period. In May 1942, when Sato was nineteen years old, she and her family (parents and younger brothers and sisters) were sent to the Japanese American internment camp at Poston, Arizona. She left the Poston Camp alone in early October 1942, only five months after *evacuation* from Sacramento, California, which was her hometown. Even though Sato entered university successfully, social discrimination restricted her social involvement, and finally she decided to volunteer in the U.S. Air Force to better her life. She served as an Air Force nurse at U.S. bases in Asian countries from 1951 to 1953.

Sato's post-internment *resettlement* as a *Nisei* woman was largely determined and shaped by her military service during the Korean War. Without the doors opened to her by her wartime service, her process of re-entry into social life as an American citizen after internment probably would have been far more difficult.

The greatest difference between female and male members of the U.S. military during the Korean War is that women in uniform took part in *feminized* duties in the military. They mainly served on home ground. Sato, while never dispatched to the Korean Peninsula, was stationed at Clark Air Force Base in the Philippines for the first six months of her service, and later was attached to the Far East Air Material Command (FEAMCOM) in Tachikawa, Japan. By the end of 1951, the FEAMCOM was the main hospital of the U.S. Air Force, where wounded soldiers from the Korean battlefield were cared for. The period of Sato's deployment from Philippines to Japan coincided with the establishment of the Air Force Medical Service, which set up the FEAMCOM as the main Air Force hospital.[31] After Sato's military service ended in 1953, she returned to her birthplace, Sacramento, and continued working as a nurse, specializing in nursing care related to ophthalmology.

In order to consider Sato's process of *resettlement,* I use *home* theory in order to examine Sato's sense of *home.* Generally, *home* indicates the *space/ place* where a person belongs.[32] For example, *home* usually conveys meanings similar to a family home, homeland, or hometown from which a person comes. However, in their collaborative work *Home*, Blunt and Dowling define it as "a *place*, a site which we live in, but more than this, home is also an idea and imaginary that is imbued with feelings"[33] ; they elaborate that "[t]hese are maybe feelings of belonging, desire and intimacy (as, for instance, in the phrase 'feeling at home,') but also [can] be feelings of fear, violence and alienation."[34] In other words, *home* is connected to one's specific identity. The *space/place* is a personal sense of the place, which is not always a real figure.

To understand Sato's *resettlement,* I first investigate her *settlement* experience before her forced World War II evacuation to a Japanese American internment camp. What was her recognition of *home* like before her internment experience? The preface of *Kiyo's Story* presents a picture of a house with Sato's family. It is titled "The Sato family's first home." Sato calls this house "our home," and the photo also shows a strawberry field among the primary images of her sense of *home.* Sato associates her *home* with happy memories.

Sato's sense of *home* also includes memories of her childhood experience. Margaret Morse explains how *home* is related to personal feelings and memory as follows:

> Feelings and memories linked to home are highly charged, if not with meaning, then with sense memories that began in childhood before the mastery of language. A fortuitous and fleeting smell, a spidery touch, a motion, a bitter taste— almost beyond our conscious ability to bid or concoct or recreate—

home is thus an evocation that is of this sensory world, ephemeral and potential in the least familiar. [35]

People are reminded of their *homes* by subtle things. For Sato, strawberry fields or strawberries serve as reminders of her *home*. Her autobiography provides a vivid account of certain childhood experiences:

> I don't know when I become aware of the world around me. I slip off my *zori* straw slippers and feel the soft spring grass under my feet. Sometimes I wander away from the strawberry field to the puddles in the neighboring property to pick tiny pink flowers. The strawberry crates are my playthings; they become a house, a table or a chair. I have one kewpie doll about as tall as my glass of milk. Mama puts the doll in her lunch crate along with a gallon of water every morning before we walk to the strawberry field. She also has a snack for me, like a box of cheese crackers, and on cold mornings, a bottle of hot chocolate wrapped up in a dish towel. [36]

When I visited Sato for my second interview in March 24, 2011, I gave her a box of chocolates as a souvenir from Japan. These were chocolate-covered strawberries produced near my hometown in Hokkaido prefecture, Japan. They were not related with her past memories at all. However, the chocolate proved to be enough to remind her of her past, as I realized during our conversation.

Sato shared her memory with me of a chocolate factory in Oslo, Norway in the mid-1950s. After Sato returned to her home in Sacramento from military service, she traveled around Europe with a friend for about six months. During her tour of Europe she picked up odd jobs to earn money to continue her travels. The Oslo chocolate factory was one of her jobs. After my interview, Sato wrote an E-mail to me and reported that she brought left-over chocolate and had shared it with her "siblings who grew up with strawberries." Finally, she remembered vividly her "home with strawberry field." [37]

Sato's images of *settlement* define her *home*. The place of *settlement* was created by her parents' generation, *Issei*, and Sato and her siblings, who were all *Nisei* children, grew up there. However, her family lost both their home and the surrounding land, and their sense of *settlement*, when forced to evacuate to the internment camp. Sato's image for *settlement* in the past is definitive of her memories of *resettlement* that are later to come. Her *settlement* experience before her internment defines the *home* that she should return to after leaving the camp.

One characteristic of Sato's wartime *resettlement* as a *Nisei* woman is that she left the camp at a very early date. Sato spent only five months in Poston Camp. As stated earlier, the duration of her stay was short compared to those experienced by other *Issei* or *Nisei*.

In addition, her experience of *resettlement* during World War II was an unusual case as a *Nisei* woman. Most *Nisei* internees who obtained early release to attend college, or to do farm work following the WRA resettlement policy for *Nisei* were *Nisei* men. Sato's early *resettlement* during World War II affected her parents' policy for their children's education. Referring to her memoir, Sato's parents hoped all their children would get higher education, and her parents were agreed to let her leave the internment camp alone. On the other hand, the previous studies of Masuda note the case of a *Nisei* woman who gave up entering university even though she got permission from both WRA and a host university, because of disagreement between her parents and another family. The woman's parents hoped the daughter would remain in the camp and take care of her brothers and sisters. Traditional domestic gender roles prevented some *Nisei* women's release from the camp in this way.

Sato was among the *Nisei* who left the camp following the WRA's *resettlement* plan at an early date. During wartime *resettlement*, about 4200 *Nisei* had left the camp by the summer of 1942. Furthermore, more than 250 additional *Nisei* had left by the end of the same year.[38] In fact, the WRA had already planned the *wartime resettlement* of Japanese Americans by April 1942 before forcing Japanese Americans to leave the West Coast, and the plan began in May 1942 in parallel with carrying out the *internment policy*. The main target of the *wartime resettlement plan* was *loyal Nisei*, especially college students and later *Nisei* recruited by the WRA for agricultural work.[39] The WRA needed *Nisei* who could demonstrate loyalty to the U. S., had never been educated in Japan, and had received admission to a university prior to leaving the internment camp.[40] Sato was one young *Nisei* who was allowed to attend university in the Midwest as demonstration of a *loyal Nisei* student by WRA policy.

However, wartime *resettlement* by the WRA prohibited Japanese Americans from "establishing a community"; they were forced to migrate to various locations in the Midwest or the East Coast. The WRA intentionally called this policy *resettlement*, in the same way the U.S. government officially named internment camps *relocation centers* instead of *internment camps.* The goal of wartime *resettlement* by the WRA was to develop government-selected "model Japanese Americans," and force them to relocate to the Midwest or the East Coast. The Japanese Americans were required by the WRA to assimilate into the "white mainstream" community.[41] Under the wartime *resettlement, Nisei* resided in locations they had never lived in before,[42] such as universities distant from their former homes, former internment camps, or agricultural areas.

Sato decided to enter college at an unfamiliar place in the state of Michigan. She believed that leaving the camp was the only way to become a "free" person even though she faced difficulties outside the camp. Her determination is reflected in the title of chapter eleven of her autobiography, "Free! First Child Released Free! Second Child Released."[43] She agreed with WRA authorities to leave the camp alone, leaving her family behind, and her decision is conveyed in the word "free," not "leave."

However, once in college, she faced several difficulties, especially financial. She also describes herself as completely exhausted. She didn't have enough time to study because her part-time job, which she needed to pay tuition, lasted more than ten hours a day. In addition, she felt that she was under a lot of pressure. She writes that she was "the first internee to be released to the state of Michigan. Upon [her] deportment depend[ed] the future release of students to Michigan."[44] In addition, "[i]t's a heavy responsibility and I take it seriously. There is no choice. I am keenly aware that one misstep and I jeopardize the future of many others."[45]

The same as Sato, all *Nisei* students were required to be role models for other Japanese Americans. According to research done by Meagan Asaka, resettled *Nisei* students were instructed to speak only English, not to talk about where they came from, and not to fraternize with other *Nisei* students. Some Japanese students strongly resisted these "rules" of the WRA, and others obeyed them.[46] It seems that Sato's thinking was somewhat different from those students. She writes that "[t]here is some comfort in knowing that I am different and that I don't have to fit certain social standards."[47] She thought of herself as an *in-between* person who lived between contrasting conditions *in* and *out* of the internment camp. She embraced her difficult situation as something that was *shikataganai* (a Japanese term meaning "a situation or results that cannot be helped").

Living on campus in Michigan was her only way of leaving the internment camp, but it was a hard time for Sato. She hoped there was some place outside the camp where she could experience a stable existence, but she could not find such a place. Her campus life was far from her *resettlement* place.

In fact, while a college student, Sato had to change her living place several times. During the semester she stayed in a dorm on campus; however, when the term ended, she had to leave campus and find a different place to stay. Because she only had permission to live in university housing, no one guaranteed her security off campus. It was a serious problem to find a safe residence during college vacation. The war in the Pacific was still underway, and racial discrimination against Japanese Americans remained rampant. While not in school, she had to migrate within the Midwest when she found a "right" place to stay. As a result, during her college years, and especially during college vacation periods, Sato had no concept of *home* and no place to call home.

Also, her concept of *home* was subject to change as she continually migrated to find places in which she could survive. In Sato's case, she led an invisible existence as a U.S. citizen, and she remained emotionally distraught over "her lost home," even though her family was able to leave the camp in fall 1943 after completing a "loyalty registration,"[48] and migrating to another to a small town named Keenesburg in Colorado. There, the family farmed sugar beets. In summer 1944, Sato visited her family in Colorado for the first time.

In *Kiyo's Story*, there is a scene where Sato's *Nisei* friend Takeo takes her to her new home in Keenesburg by his car from the nearest—but very far—bus station in Colorado. Sato was disappointed to see the temporary family home. She recalls her conversation with Takeo in the following excerpt. "'We're almost there,' he [Takeo] assures me, as we drive down a long, narrow dirt road. What terrible place have they moved to?"[49]

Analyzing the scene of the family's *relocation* to Colorado, it is understood that the family home in Keenesburg was temporary and not a new *settling* place for her, either. It was impossible to forget her original home in Sacramento, even though Sato's family *resettlement* was a successful case of wartime post-internment *resettlement*.

On December 12, 1944, in *Ex parte Endo*, the U.S. Supreme Court decided "that the WRA could not detain U.S. citizens who were shown to be loyal, effectively ending incarceration."[50] As a result, ten internment camps were closed by 1946. In January 1945, when Japanese American internees were permitted to return to their homes on the West Coast, Sato and her family decided to return to Sacramento immediately.

The WRA's mission, which was to drive Japanese Americans from the West Coast and spread them all over the country, was finally ended. However, the WRA's mission was partly a success. It drastically changed Japanese American demographics in various regions in the U.S. After internment ended, and the camps were closed, some Japanese Americans never returned to the West Coast and decided to *resettle* in the Midwest or on the East Coast. There were about 57,000 former internees on the West Coast before the summer of 1946. The number included not only those returning directly from the camp, but also those moving from the Midwest or the East Coast *resettlement places.*[51]

Sato's family returned to their original home in Sacramento, California, from the temporary home in Keenesburg, Colorado, in spring 1945.[52] Sato went to California by herself in order to prepare for her family's arrival on January 14, 1945. It was only a few weeks after the *Ex parte Endo* decision was issued. Sato describes her helplessness and loneliness upon embarking on her journey to return to her hometown. "My train heads straight west into what was the 'restricted zone' from where we were evicted. Terrible thoughts keep crowding into my brain. At least, we have a safe place now on the sugar beet farm. Are we better off staying in Colorado?"[53]

However, on the way to California, Sato felt happy and exuberant when she saw the scenery of California from the train's window. "I awaken as the train slowly climbs the wintry, dreary side of Sierra Nevada Mountains. We finally hit the summit and descend into California. I want to yell to the whole world, 'I am home!'"[54] Thus, she depicts her feeling of happiness to return to her original, loving *home.*

As the war against Japan was winding down, in California there were several incidents of violence and rejection movements against Japanese American former internees.[55] To return to the West Coast was a risky endeavor for Japanese internees. Sato's family had already built up their lives in Colorado. So they had another choice; to remain in Colorado after the war ended or to stay in Colorado much longer and return to their home after hate movements against Japanese Americans in California subsided. Why did they return at such an early time in spite of the risky circumstances surrounding Japanese Americans? In *Kiyo's Story,* it seems that the most important reason why Sato and her family tried to return to Sacramento at such an early time comes from emotional attachment to their California home, rather than economic reasons. Sato discovered that her Sacramento home was now occupied by strangers without their permission, and their former *home* was gone. Moreover, a part of the house had been damaged by a plane accident. She writes, "I can't believe what I am *not* seeing."[56]

After Sato coped with her family's housing problems, her main *resettlement* issues shifted to finding a way to get involved in American society as a *Nisei* woman. Getting a university education and hunting for a job where she could earn enough to be an independent person now became her chief priorities. Analyzing Sato's process of returning to her home in California, her idea of *resettlement* is not complete when she returns *to* her friendly and original *home* in Sacramento. Her real *resettlement* as a *Nisei* woman started from this period onward. Her purpose in *resettlement* has changed from coming back to *home* in the West Coast to integrating herself into American society as a *Nisei.*

SATO'S MILITARY SERVICE
AND THE CONDITION OF CITIZENSHIP

The Way to the Military Service and Ending of the Resettlement

And now, let us discuss Sato's military service during the Korean War. In order to end her *resettlement,* Sato needed to find the *right* place to live as a U.S. citizen within the U.S. This *place* has two meanings—both spatial and social—so much of the discussion will center on her process of obtaining *social* place within the U.S. during the 1950s, a process certainly facilitated by her military service. Sato could join the Air Force even though she was a *minority* woman in the U.S. in this period because her own decision operated positively within, and was welcomed by, U.S. society. Acts of gender and ethnic inclusion of 1948 were also operating in her case.

In 1947, Sato finally could enter a nursing school to get a master's degree in nursing. In fact, she had previously been rejected in 1945 by all nursing schools for *racial* reasons.[57] Even in 1947, only the Cadet Nurse Corps program of Western Reserve University (WRU) accepted her. Sato was discriminated against because of her race—she was a former American enemy, a Japanese American. Then, the Pacific War was over, Japan was totally defeated and would soon become an important sub-partner of the U.S. in the Far East. At this point, Sato could manage to enter nursing school.

However, the most significant differences between Sato's case and those of male soldiers were that her case was affected by U.S. governmental policies concerning not only racial issues but also gender issues. In short, the process of her entrance into university was affected by the changing working style of U.S. women during wartime. She entered the Cadet Nurse program of WRU, a system that arose during World War II. The Nurse Training Act was passed by Congress in July 1943, and the school program ended in 1948. The United States Cadet Nurse Corps was created under the organization of the United States Public Health Service (USPHS). Senator Frances Payne Bolton (Republican, Ohio) made great efforts to pass this law. In fact, the system of the Cadet Nurse Corps drastically changed the education and training system for nursing in the U.S. It was the largest scholarship program for women students in nursing in U.S. history.

After graduating WRU in 1951, Sato volunteered as a member of the AFNC. After she trained for half a year at Camp Shelby in Mississippi, she was sent to Air Force bases in Asia, both in the Philippines and in Japan.[58] Sato finished her military service abroad and returned safely home to Sacramento from the Air Force base in Japan. For Sato, this represented the end of her *resettlement*. Being a servicewoman changed her social status drastically. Once she was a former internee, but now she was an American veteran. She was finally recognized as a *proper American citizen* by the U. S. because she had served and shown her total loyalty to the nation. Like the military service of *Nisei men*, Sato's volunteering in the AFNC during the Korean War allowed her to rise above the difficult social position of being a former internee.

In addition, unlike male combat soldiers, Sato did not experience the hardships of the battlefield. She was stationed at U.S. military bases in Asian countries dedicated to medical care. This is one of the reasons she regarded her military service positively. It seems that her service experience was not a traumatic event for her. In *Kiyo's Story*, Sato writes that the only free time she had in Japan was when she visited her grandmother in Chiba, where Sato's father (Shinji) was born and had lived until he immigrated to California at the age of fourteen. Sato could find her *Nisei* roots by visiting her *Issei* father's Japanese birthplace, and she could ponder her ethnic roots positively. She describes the touching meeting she and her father had with her Japanese grandmother:

> I sit by her cradling her bony fingers with both my hands. How hard these hands have worked; how deeply this small body has worried and worked to keep her family intact! How desperate was she, the mother who would tell her young son; "*koko he kaette kuru na, Shinji,*" trusting that hope for her son's future lay in America. Don't come back here, she had whispered, her heart aching that it would be the last time she would ever see her son. [59]

Since the Japanese Americans' evacuation and internment during the Pacific War had begun, Sato's Japanese ethnic roots were only a source of trouble. However, she began to regard her ethnic heritage more positively when she visited her grandmother and other relatives in Japan.

As a result, when she returned to her home in Sacramento upon completing her military service, she was able to succeed at reintegrating herself into American society. For example, in the section of her autography titled "1956, Sacramento, California," she describes how the social situation of herself and her siblings became better. "Happy times prevail. Children [Sato and her brothers and sisters] continue school. Five sons and a daughter [Sato] return home safely from military service. Each of us pursues our own goal." [60] Thus, even though Sato's *Nisei* status jeopardized her U.S. citizenship during the Pacific War, she was now willingly seizing the opportunity to claim the benefits that came with being a veteran of the Korean War period.

Also, at the same time, she could reconfirm that her *home* as a *Nisei* was certainly in Sacramento, even though she had previously experienced exclusion. Finally, she gained confidence in her ethnicity as a *Nisei* even though discrimination against Japanese Americans still remained in her birthplace in California after the Pacific War ended and her family resettled in Sacramento.

Sato's experiences during military service were enough to finish her *resettlement*. After her service ended, Sato's return to Sacramento became a second experience of returning home. Once she had returned home as a former internee, and now she returned as a U.S. veteran. In the interim, her social status in U.S. society had greatly changed.

I have reviewed Sato's *resettlement* and military service in Korea as a case study of a *Nisei* woman in uniform. The *resettlement* was a series of experiences involving migration and changing residency of Japanese American former internees within the U.S. Sato's *resettlement* was composed of several experiences that recast her existence in U.S. society as a legitimate American citizen after her internment.

A *NISEI* WOMAN IN THE U.S. MILITARY
DURING THE COLD WAR

Finally, I will focus on Sato's military service in detail again and rethink the successful elements of a *Nisei* woman's *resettlement,* discussing the conditions of a *Nisei* woman working in the U.S. military during the 1950s. What kind of difficulties did Sato encounter during her military service in the 1950s? During my interviews with her, she stated that serving as a member of the AFNC was a "smooth experience" for her. What explains this "smooth experience" for Sato?

One reason is improved legal conditions for Japanese Americans after World War II. However, social circumstances among Japanese Americans were still hard in fact. In addition, though the 1950s were known for being a *conservative* era, the social roles of all U.S. women changed. In her study, Elaine Tyler May has suggested that U.S. women in the 1950s were subjected to "containment at home."[61] This means that U.S. women tended to return to domestic roles, to become housewives, and did not work outside, in contrast to the World War II period. A few years after *total war*, the U.S. labor market no longer needed women to fill out its workforce. Despite this reversion to a more conservative and domesticated role for women, why could Sato get jobs, both civilian and military, during the 1950s, even though she was a *minority* woman? Because she became a nurse.

In the early Cold War era, working as a nurse was seen as a suitable profession for a working woman in U.S. society. The studies of Jane Sherron-DuHart mention that becoming a nurse or teacher was popular among college-educated women in the 1950s.[62] These occupations were treated in the U.S. as *feminized* jobs. This idea also operated in the military. Working as a nurse-soldier in the AFNC was considered a *proper* gender role for a service woman. As the AFNC was an all-woman-unit until reorganized by the Air Force in 1955, becoming a fighting-nurse let U.S. military women pursue careers as legitimate soldiers while keeping their *femininity*.

The argument of the feminist political scientist Cynthia Enloe helps in understanding Sato's military case in the Korean War. Enloe examined the case of women in the military during the Gulf War and argues that becoming a professional permitted a woman to go into the military:

> For violent sacrifice and state-disciplined service have been imagined in American culture to be masculine domains. What reconciles the unresolved national debate over women's proper place in wartime with the cultural inclination to associate true citizenship with militarized sacrifice? It may be professionalization. If American citizen-soldiering became professionalized—if it could be liberated from its traditional need to be associated with minuteman amateurism—*and* if professionalization could bestow on American notions of femininity a new coat of protective respectability, then perhaps women could

attain first-class citizenship without jeopardizing the still-gendered political culture.[63]

Enloe argues that women were permitted to approach military service owing to their professionalism, and finally they could get *first-class citizenship* in return,[64] the same as men in service. This kind of logic could be applied to Sato's service during the Korean War. Also, this was why members of the AFNC were admitted to regular units in the Air Force in this period. They were specialists of nursing.

Following Enloe's argument, there are two possible reasons why members of the AFNC were permitted to become regular soldiers, who could partly obtain veterans benefits the same as male combat soldiers after returning from service. The first reason was that the AFNC presented the role of a *feminized* professional in the military. The second reason was that the presence of female nurse-soldiers on home ground was welcomed in the military society because their presence highlighted the role of the male combat soldiers on the battlefield. The woman nurse-soldier cared for male combat soldiers, and conversely, the AFNC units observed the *masculinity* of male combat soldiers. Sato became a member of the AFNC, and took a *feminized* role in military society. Finally, Sato's professional occupation in the nurse corps allowed her to become a professional military person.

When the U.S. government allowed *Nisei* men to enlist in the army starting in 1943, military service was the one of the definitive ways of proving loyalty to the U.S., and also demonstrating fulfillment of one's duty as a U.S. citizen. *Nisei's* demonstration of their loyalty to the country through their service meant that they dedicated their lives to the country, which then made it possible for *Nisei* to be re-admitted as full-fledged citizens in the U.S. This is the thought of the *citizen-soldier,* widely used in U.S. society from America's earliest moments. Sato's military service followed the model of the *citizen-soldier* as it applied to female soldiers during the Korean War period.

Rethinking Sato's case, she was once a *Nisei* woman, who experienced subjugation for both ethnic and gender reasons, but she was finally permitted to take up the role of someone serving in the military, and in turn this made it possible for her to seek *full-citizenship* using her military dedication and credentials. Sato's experiences as a member of the AFNC in the Korean War period promoted her social re-entry into U.S. society after she returned from the military. Sato volunteered to become a U.S. Air Force nurse during the Korean War. She assumed a positive and *proper* gender role as a woman in the military in this period.

But, for women in uniform in this period, taking a *proper* gender role in military society—usually thought of as an "all-male-society"—and pursuing careers as female soldiers did not bring only advantages for them. Later female soldiers gained additional access to the battlefield and faced an increased likelihood of death than before. Women soldiers started to be sent to battlefields from the Vietnam War era on a full scale. Sato, a racial *minority* woman who accepted her gender role in the military during the 1950s, became one of the elements facilitating the next generation's greater embrace of women in the military.

CONCLUSION

In the early years of the Cold War era, *Nisei* service in the Korean War was welcomed by the U.S. government because this service could represent the loyalty of *racial minorities* to the U.S. Reviewing Sato's case, due to her decision to become a nurse, a *Nisei* woman in U.S. society in the early 1950s could become an independent person after proving her loyalty through volunteering for military service. Becoming a nurse was a suitable job for a woman outside the home according to social standards then prevailing in the U.S.

She sought *full-citizenship* using the same logic employed by *Nisei* men who served in the U.S. military. The U.S. government promoted the image of the U.S. as a *liberal* country in this period. Thus, even though Sato was a woman, her own decision to become a nurse-soldier was supported as a demonstration of loyalty and patriotism.

Sato's voluntary military experience facilitated her social involvement as a *Nisei*. After she completed her military service and returned home, Sato could more comfortably embrace her *resettlement* as a Japanese American. During the early years of the Cold War, social norms of gender and sexuality became conservative and more rigid. What became the norm in U.S. society was also the operative norm in the U.S. military. Therefore, the division of labor by gender role between men and women was clearly defined by military duty. And it was affected by differences in gender roles, regardless of whether someone served at or near the Korean War battlefront or in safer areas.

In order for Sato to survive her hard life as a *Nisei* after the internment era, she chose to become a nurse and voluntarily joined the AFNC during the Korean War. Because she served at U.S. bases in both the Philippines and Japan, Sato could achieve her *resettlement* as a *Nisei* woman serving in the Korean War period. Though she was under disadvantageous conditions in U.S. society in those days, she could enter the social mainstream relatively easily because her social role in the military was within the contemporary range of images of women working outside of the home. Thus, her decision was suitable for the style of the 1950s, a style that supported *militarized citizenship* and engendering of the military.

Finally, how might this study be applied to future studies? Examination of *Nisei* military service in the Korean War and the process of *resettlement* during the 1950s will lead next to discussions of the origins of the *model minority* of Japanese Americans, which appeared widely in the U.S. in the 1960s. In subsequent studies, I will analyze the *resettlement* processes of *Nisei* male soldiers who served at the battlefront and how their service images contributed to creation of the myth of a Japanese American *model minority* in later periods. The Korean War generally has been named the *forgotten war* in American society; however, it was not forgotten at all. Reconsidering the *resettlement* of *Nisei* and their citizenship status during the 1950s, military service during the Korean War was also a significant element, and it reveals additional social connections of *Nisei* in this period.

NOTES

1. This chapter is the revised version of my conference paper, "Experiences of Japanese American Soldiers in the Korean War from Gender and Ethnic Perspectives: The Case of a *Nisei* Woman in the U.S. Air Force Nurse Corps" presented at the *Osaka University International Symposium, Legacies of World War II Part 1*, at Osaka University, October 31, 2014. The early idea for this chapter comes from my Ph.D. dissertation, *"Nisei* Soldiers in the Korean War: Gender and Ethnic Perspectives on the Service Experience during the Early Cold War," submitted to Ochanomizu University in September 2014. I deeply appreciate for people and institutions that support my research project below: Ms. Kiyo Sato, agreed to be interviewed and kindly gave important information of her life history; Research Grants from the Shibusawa Fund for Ethnological Studies, the Tokai Foundation for Gender Studies, and the Research Grant for the Ph.D. Program Student in Ochanomizu University. I also thank Dr. Shuichi Takebayashi (Doshisha University) for giving me helpful advice to revise this paper.

2. In this chapter, the term *Japanese American* indicates all people who identified their ethnic origin as Japanese or whose ancestors originally came from Japan.

3. The U.S. government called these camps *relocation centers*. However, in this chapter, considering the huge damage to Japanese Americans, I refer to them as *concentration camps* or *internment camps*.

4. See Arthur A. Hansen, "Resettlement: A Neglected Link in Japanese America's Narrative Chain," Regenerations Oral History Project: Japanese American Families, Communities, and Civil Rights Era: Los Angeles Region, accessed July 30, 2015, http://content.cdlib.org/view?docId=ft358003z1;NAAN=13030&doc.view=frames&chunk.id=d0e566&toc.depth=1&toc.id=&brand=calisphere.

5. For example, see Hansen (ibid.); Naoko Masuda, *"Nikkei Americajin no Saiteijyu- seisaku: Dainiji Sekaitaisenchu no America-ka to Nichibei Identity no Hojino Soukoku ni Tsuite no Ichi Kosatsu,"* [Resettlement Policy of Japanese Americans: Americanization during World War II and Japanese American Struggle of Dual Identity between the U.S. and Japan], *Seigakuin University General Research Institute,* vol. 35 (2006), pp. 487–514; Gary Y. Okihiro, *Storied Lives: Japanese American Students and World War II* (Seattle: University of Washington Press, 1999); and Lane R. Hiyabayashi, *Japanese American Resettlement through the Lens: Hikaru Iwasaki and the WRA's Photographic Section, 1943–1945* (Boulder [CO]: The University Press of Colorado, 2009).

6. Kiyo Sato, *Kiyo's Story: A Japanese American Families' Quest for the American Dream* (New York: SOHO Press, 2009). The first edition of this book was published as *Dandelion through the Crack* in 2007.

7. See the chapter of "Interview" by Ikuya Sato entitled *Fieldwork: Sho wo Motte Machi he Deyoh* [Fieldwork: Go outside with Books] (Tokyo: Shinyo-sha, 2008), pp. 191–98. In the "structured interview" or "formal interview," the interviewee is given a well-prepared questionnaire by the interviewer before being interviewing. In contrast, the "non-structured interview" or "informal interview" does not provide a formal questionnaire. For example, the "participant

observation" is one of the methods in the "informal interview". The "semi-structured-style" is situated between formal and informal interviews. In my case, I did not use a formal question-naire for interviewees, and I ask interviewees to speak freely without time-limit about both my prepared and non-prepared questions for them.

8. Robert M. Wada, *From Internment, to Korea, to Solitude: Memoir of Robert M. Wada Nisei Child of a WWII Japanese America Internment Camp and Later a Marine Corps Veteran of the Korean War* (Charleston [SC]: Booksurge, 2009).

9. See "Asian Americans in the Korean War," Department of Defense 60th Anniversary of Korean War Commemoration Committee, accessed June 9, 2015, http://www.koreanwar60 .com/asian-americans-korean-war-0, and Robert M. Wada and Japanese American Korean War Veterans Inc. *Americans of Japanese Ancestry in the Korean War: Stories of Those Who Served,* Norio Uyematsu ed. (Fullerton, Paragon Agency Publishers, 2009), viii.

10. Wada and Japanese American Korean War Veterans Inc., viii.

11. Undocumented interview with Robert M. Wada by the author.

12. See Edwin Nakasone, *The Nisei Soldier: Historical Essays on World War II and the Korean War* (White Bear Lake [MN]: J-press, 1999) and Chapter 11 of Yukiko Yanagida. *Nisei-heishi Gekitono Kiroku: Nikkei Americajin no Dainiji Sekaitaisen* [Record of the *Nisei* Soldier's Heavy Battle: Japanese Americans under World War II] (Tokyo: Shincho-sha, 2012).

13. Michi Nishimura Weglyn, *Years of Infamy: The Untold Story of America's Concentra-tion Camps* (Seattle [WA]: University of Washington Press, 2003), p. 36.

14. See Weglyn, *Years of Infamy*, p.136 and Report of the Commission on Wartime Reloca-tion and Internment of Civilians, *Personal Justice Denied* (2nd ed., Washington D.C. and San Francisco: The Civil Liberties Public Education Fund and Seattle and London: University of Washington Press, 2000), pp. 13–15. The WRA "tests" every internee over seventeen years-old to determine loyalty to the U.S. prior to selecting "resettlement internees" and *Nisei* draftees for military service.

15. Takashi Fujitani, *Race for Empire: Koreans as Japanese and Japanese as Americans during World War II* (Berkeley [CA]: University of California Press, 2011), pp.5–6.

16. Hansen wrote in the late 1980s that "the resettlement experience of Japanese Americans has been relegated to the margins of scholarly literature and popular memory, not only outside, but also within Japanese America." In fact, since the time Hansen made that comment several studies that have touched on Japanese American *resettlement* generally envelop this issue in the study of World War II internment.

17. Andrew Huebner, *The Warrior Image: Soldiers in American Culture from the Second World War to the Vietnam Era* (Chapel Hill [NC]: The University of North Carolina Press, 2008), p. 132.

18. Based on two interviews with Veteran #1(anonymous). These interviews were con-ducted by the author with veteran #1, in November 2008 and September 2009.

19. From the interviews with veteran #1.

20. From two interviews with veteran #2. These interviews were conducted by the author with veteran #2, in November 2009 and March 2011.

21. Wada and Japanese American Korean War Veterans Inc., *Americans of Japanese Ances-try*, p. 190.

22. Assistant Secretary for Planning and Analysis, Office of Program and Data Analyses, "Data on Veterans of the Korean War" (United States Department of Veterans Affairs, June 2000), accessed April 15, 2015, http://www1.va.gov/vetdata/docs/SpecialReports/KW2000 .pdf.

23. Jennifer A. Delton, *Rethinking the 1950s: How Anticommunism and the Cold War Made America Liberal* (NY: Cambridge University Press, 2013), pp. 1–4.

24. Public Law 625.

25. During World War II, other groups of Asian Americans, such as Chinese and Filipinos, also joined the military. About13,000 Chinese people served in the U.S. military. A few of Korean ancestry also joined. Most Chinese, Filipino, and Korean soldiers joined racially inte-grated units; however, a segregated unit of Chinese Americans existed in the Air Force.

26. In my dissertation, (see endnote1), I also discussed gender roles and sexualities of *Nisei* male soldiers in the 1950s.

27. October 28, 1953 in the *New York Times.*

28. See "Fact Sheet: Operation Big and Little Switch," Korean War 60th Anniversary Memorial Project by State of New Jersey, Department of Military and Veterans Affairs, 2010, accessed July 20, 2015, http://www.nj.gov/military/korea/factsheets/opswitch.html and "Defectors: By Mutual Consent," an article in *Time* magazine, July 15, 1966, accessed July 30, 2-15, http://content.time.com/time/magazine/article/0,9171,835998,00.html.

29. Robert G Lee. *Orientals: Asian American in Popular Culture* (Philadelphia[PA]: Temple University Press, 1995), p. 145.

30. Norio Akashi and Iino Masako, *Ethnic America: Taminzokukokka ni okeru Togo no Genjitsu* [Ethnic America: The Fact of Integration in the Multiracial Nation] (Tokyo: Yuhikaku, 2000), p. 202.

31. For a brief history of the AFNC, see Sharon A. Vario, "History of the United States Air Force Nurse Corps: 1949-1954," (Dissertation, University of San Diego, 1998).

32. Doreen Massey, "Living in Wythenshawe," in *The Unknown City: Contesting Architecture and Social Space*, ed. by Iain Bordon et al. (Cambridge [MA]: MIT Press, 2001), pp. 459–75.

33. Alison Blunt and Robyn Dowling, *Home* (Oxfordshire, Abingdon U.K.: Routledge, 2006), p. 2.

34. Ibid and Alison Blunt and Ann Varley, "Introduction: Geographies of home." *Geographies of home* 11 (2004), pp. 3–6.

35. Margaret Morse, "home: smell, taste, posture, gleam" in *Home, Exile, Homeland: Film, Media, and the Politics of Place*, ed. by Hamid Naficy (NY: Routledge, 1999), pp. 63–75.

36. Sato, *Kiyo's Story*, pp. 35–36.

37. I quote the phrase from Sato's e-mail correspondence with me dated April 1, 2011.

38. *Personal Justice Denied,* pp. 180–81.

39. See *Personal Justice Denied*, pp. 180–84. The WRA had already planned the *resettlement* of Japanese Americans by April 1942 before forcing Japanese Americans to leave the West Coast, and the plan was started from in May in parallel with carrying out the *internment policy.* The main target of the *resettlement* plan was *loyal Nisei,* especially college students. Later the WRA also recruited *Nisei* for employment as agricultural workers.

40. Masuda, *Nikkei America Jin no Saiteijyu Seisaku*, p. 487.

41. Ibid., p. 514.

42. Sato, *Kiyo's Story*, p. 448.

43. Ibid., p. 173.

44. Ibid., p. 189.

45. Ibid.

46. Meagan Asaka, "Resettlement," *Densho Encyclopedia*, last modified July 2, 2012. accessed July 30, 2015. http://encyclopedia.densho.org/Resettlement.

47. Ibid., p. 185.

48. See Weglyn, *Years of Infamy*, p. 136 and *Personal Justice Denied*, pp. 13–15.

49. Sato, *Kiyo's Story*, p. 206.

50. *Personal Justice Denied ,* p. 236.

51. Masuda, *Nikkei Americajin no Saiteijyu-seisaku*, p. 13.

52. Sato, *Kiyo's Story,* p. 245.

53. Ibid., p. 229.

54. Ibid., p. 230.

55. Noriko Shimada, *Nikkei Americajin no Taiheiyou Sensou [Pacific War of Japanese Americans]* (Tokyo: Liber Press, 1995), pp. 136–42.

56. Sato, *Kiyo's Story*, p. 256. Italic in the original.

57. Ibid., pp. 200–201.

58. Ibid., p. 280.

59. Ibid., p. 286.

60. Ibid., p. 291.

61. Elaine Tyler May, *Homeward Bound: American Families in the Cold War Era*, 2nd ed. (NY: Basic Books, 1999), pp. 10–29.

62. Jane Sherron DeHart, "Containment at Home" in ed. by Peter J. Kuznick and James Gilbert, *Rethinking Cold War Culture* ed. by Peter J. Kuznick and James Gilbert (Washington: Smithsonian Institution Press, 2001), pp. 124–55.

63. Cynthia Enloe, *The Morning After* (Berkeley [CA]: University of California Press, 1993), p. 202.

64. For a discussion of soldier's citizenship, see James Burk, "Citizenship Status and Military Service: The Quest for Inclusion by Minorities and Conscientious Objection." *Armed Forces & Society* Vol. 21 No. 4 (Summer 1995), pp.503–29.

Chapter Three

Towards a More Amicable Asia-Pacific

Rethinking Japan's Relations with the US and China[1]

Victor Teo, Assistant Professor,
The University of Hong Kong

It is becoming exceeding difficult as a political scientist to write on relations between the countries in East Asia without offending some sensibilities. This even more true when we consider the relationship between Japan and the United States or Japan and her closest neighbor, the People's Republic of China.

The narratives in the media—both in Japan and internationally gives us a broad picture of the perceived developments in Japan-China and Japan-US relations. Day in day out, we are told by the Western and Japanese media reports that that Chinese naval vessels and airplanes are infringing Japanese airspace[2] , and that Hong Kong and Taiwanese activists are confronting Japan Maritime Defense forces on the high seas[3] in their bid to sail to the Senkaku Islands. Concurrently, this news are echoed across the Chinese-speaking world a similar manner but the message is reversed: Japanese navy ships and vessels are blocking Chinese boats from reaching their rightful territory in the East China Sea.[4] International reports also highlight the United States' position on the East Asia: the Americans urged China and Japan to resolve their differences over the East China Seas dispute peacefully[5] but at the same time reminded the world that the US-Japan Security alliance covers Senkaku/Diaoyu Islands situation.[6] In particular, the international media (dominantly the Western and Japanese media) focused on the acts of friendship between the Japan and the United States. In particular, the reports celebrated US involvement in Japanese affairs—ranging from rescue efforts during the Fukushima disaster to the good done by the US-Japan Security alliance in East China Sea. In contrast, the coverage on Sino-Japanese relations is not that positive. Japanese and Chinese scholars often argue loudly at international conferences, necessitated by personal ambitions, public expectations and nationalistic instincts.[7]

If one were to infer from these reports, then one's natural conclusions about Japan's foreign relations should fall around these presumptions: First, China is now Japan's number one foreign policy challenge. The People's Republic is officially a new security threat[8] —from conventional military sense to non-traditional dimensions that include food safety, organized crime and health crisis like the SARS episode in 2003. Second, the US-Japan alliance stands at the forefront of the challenges posed to Japan, especially in terms of handling the "China Threat". It provides a shield against aggression and a blanket of assurance for Japan's Asian neighbors as it sought to "normalize" her security and foreign policy posture. Like the six decades before, the US-Japan alliance is a panacea and cure all for this. Third, the over-the-horizon forecast of Sino-Japanese relations is bleak, with little or no prospect of a natural recovery. This is a now a "historic" truth, and given the wars that these two neighbors had fought, diplomatic niceties is not enough to give the veneer to gloss over these tensions that these two competing hegemons have.[9]

Three important sets of questions then become immediately apparent. First, given Japan's tremendous challenges at home, to what extent is her relationship with China her number one challenge in the foreseeable future? Secondly, is the United States alliance with Japan the entire answer to Japan's future foreign and security problems? Third, would that necessarily preclude Japan from working together with China in a non-economic realm since the US-Japan security alliance bind these two countries together? In other words, is there a way out for stalemate in Sino-Japanese Relations and what would this actually mean for Japan's alliance with the United States? How would China and Japan manage their relations for the foreseeable future, given the difficult impetus that this may mean for their foreign relations?

This chapter makes three arguments. First, Japan's foreign policy challenges lie in managing her relations not only with China but also the United States. These two sets of relations could be cultivated independently, and in order to ensure that Sino-Japanese relations develops on an even keel—Japan needs to fundamentally rethink her relations with the United States and how it affects co-operation with other powers—notably China. The United States remains a problem as much as it is a solution for Japan's foreign policy in the long run.

Second, it is entirely possible for both Japan and China to work together under certain circumstances. Whilst often constrained by the geopolitics and the mechanics of US-Japan security treaty, one possible way for China and Japan to work together is perhaps to look at opportunities beyond the Asia-

Pacific. In particular, one area that could be considered is in the provision of an international public good in a region where both countries do not perceive the stakes to be a zero-sum game. This sort of co-operation builds confidence and trust. The challenge is how to operationalise this, and prove to people of both nations that this is not something that lies only in the realm of imagination.

Third, East Asia can only become a more harmonious region if and only if Chinese and Japanese politicians consider the stakes more carefully than what they have done in previous years. In particular, as China strives to maintain the trajectory of her strategic ascendance, and Japan the momentum of her normalization, Tokyo and Beijing must avoid hegemonic contention we see so often manifesting in regional issues. The tricky part is how initiatives get off the ground given the political minefield and the hostile environment. If the solution cannot be found at the governmental level, perhaps it needs to come from the people themselves—starting from the academia. Scholars have a professional responsibility to confront bigotry, and to ensure that Japanese and Chinese people live in peace and prosperity for the foreseeable future.

JAPAN'S FOREIGN POLICY AT CROSSROADS: DOMESTIC AND EXTERNAL SOURCES FOR NORMALIZATION

Today's Japan faces an incredible slew of domestic challenges that threatens the very essence of the Japanese way of life. Through fortunate geopolitical circumstances, shrewd economic planning and good fortitude, Japan's economic miracle has seen the living standards on a per capita basis. Japanese average household net-adjusted disposable income per capita is USD $25,066 a year, more than the OECD average of USD$23,938 a year.[10] Over the next four decades, the number of people over 65 years of age will increase from approximately 27 million in 2007 to 35.8 million in 2050 based on medium projection, and their share of the total population will increase from increase from 21 per cent to 35 per cent. As the country in the region with the largest share of its population aged over 65 years, further ageing is therefore expected from 24 per cent in 2012 to 37 per cent in 2050.[11] The projected difficulty from this demographic challenge[12] would impact upon Japan's workforce and military force requirements. As the population ages, there will be more and more elderly retiring to depending on a shrinking younger work force. By 2015, it is estimated that one quarter of Japan's population will be elderly.[13] This caused considerable problems in Japan as up to 2000, Japan did not have social care for the elderly. There were widespread reports of neglect and abuse[14] as well as reports of elderly staying in hospitals simply for care rather than because they were sick. In relative terms, by 2060, Japan's population will fall by a third, and 40% of those people will be 65 will be older[15]. South Korea will rate slightly higher than Japan, with slightly over 40% of people in the same bracket, and China at 28%.[16]

Japan's economic stagnation since the 1990s had created intrinsic and extrinsic standards problems. The ability of Tokyo to fund health and social programs is intimately linked to the health of Japan's economy. With a projected increase in defense spending set to come, it becomes questionable if Japan is able to maintain very high standards & cost of living for a largely aged population. The Japanese government is trying to reinvigorate its economy by engaging in quantitative easing on an unprecedented scale. In implementing Abenomics, Japan runs the risk of higher interest rates driven, making debt servicing of Japanese bonds unserviceable.[17] It is clear that the current Prime Minister would rather take the risk than allow Japan to slide to a slow and long drawn decline. Initial results and public opinion seem to indicate that the Prime Minister has received good support.

Prime Minister Abe however did not only take risks in economics. Like his LDP predecessors[18] from 2000 onwards, the *Kantei* is leading Japan down unconventional paths in terms of foreign policy. The 1st July 2014 re-interpretation of Japan's Constitution is a major political victory for Prime Minister Abe—signifying a milestone in Japan's struggle to come to terms with the foreign policy legacies established during the post war era.[19] This is part of a broader effort that Japanese Prime Ministers, starting from the mid-1990s have been working towards in trying to change Japan into a more "normal" state. Three important challenges that have emanated over the last two decades have prompted Japan to rethink and re-evaluate her foreign policy posture in order for Japan to become a more "normal" nation.

The first comes from a deep search from within Japan in the aftermath of the 1990 Gulf War led by the United States. Despite having forked out USD$5 billion as contributions towards the first Gulf War, Japan was shocked as she recovered from criticisms from the international community.[20] Japanese elites embarked on deep soul searching over what could possibly constitute meaningful "contribution" given the constraints placed on Japan constitutionally and politically. As Japan has focused principally on "peace" as a concept throughout the post-War period, it had a difficulty period of adjustment despite pressure from the United States for Japan to do more for her defense.

The second comes from a deep sense of frustration, not only with the economic stagnation, but also with the rise of a generation that is confounded with unresolved issues of the past. Young Japanese people do not understand what it is that Korea and Chinese want from them—be it over history, war-time compensation or apologies. Certainly like the younger generation in Germany, the younger Japanese are weary of what they perceive as incessant demands from the Chinese and Koreans. Due to this attitude, they are being cast as unrepentant and militaristic. This becomes exceedingly frustrating for them as it jars with their self-image and prevailing social ideals. Rightly or wrongly, many Japanese politicians have capitalized on this sense and incorporated into their agenda and resultant policies have become relatively hawkish.

The third comes from an overwhelming sense insecurity driven by the possibility of the prospects that the strategic and economic rise of China will ebb the influence of the United States and Japan. This probably is the most worrying facet of recent developments for Japan—as it has never ever seen the like in recent history. Strategically, what worries many is that East Asia has never seen a strong Japan and a strong China co-exist in recent history. Assuming that current growth trajectory continues, Japan perceives that not only is China closing the gap but will in the near future have abilities (strategically and economically) that both Japan and the United States cannot balance. Tokyo is in fact in extremely anxious to sustain the gap over her own abilities to keep up and balance the projected trajectory of China's rise (or the consequences of its failure to rise).

PERCEIVED THREATS FROM PRC AND DPRK: EXTERNAL DRIVERS FOR JAPAN'S NORMALIZATION

North Korea and China has emerged to become important issue areas that have intensified the normalization debate in Japan over the last two decades. Whilst the scope of the normalization debate is wide ranging, covering topics from reforms over the Constitution, to Japanese military deployment to the overhauling of legislation concerning the use of force, a major impetus for driving the debate is the sense of threat that Japan perceive from two of her closest neighbors. From 1995 onwards, Japan began to have severe disagreements with China over a series of issues. The list of issues is long: over China's nuclear tests (1995);[21] over China's perceived intimidation of Taiwan over their first presidential elections with the missile tests in 1996/1997;[22] over the renewal of the US-Japan Security alliance in 1997;[23] over President Jiang Zemin criticism of the Japan over issues of history and Japan's refusal to give a written apology (1998);[24] over alleged Chinese naval incursions into Japanese territorial waters (1999);[25] the trade war over Japanese automotive and Chinese tatami (straw) in 2000,[26] and contestation over East China Sea gas deposits from 2000 onwards.[27] There are of course almost year tensions over issues to do with the burden of history; the Senkaku/Diaoyu disputes and the dispute over East China Sea gas deposits onwards.

The *Kantei*[28] and the Defense Ministry in Tokyo however was cautious in pointing out China as an explicit threat initially. The 1996 White paper first stipulated that certain Chinese actions needed to be monitored closely, such as the modernization of her nuclear forces and professionalization of her armed services. By 2000, Japan's Japan Defense Agency had explicitly noted that Japan lies with China's missile range and by 2004, Japan's white paper has identified potential scenarios which China might attach Japan.[29] With each subsequent year, China's role as a threat to Japan has become naturalized.

Compared to China, Japan was much more forthright regarding the threat posed by the DPRK. From the mid-1990s when the DPRK was facing its hardest challenge posed by the famine (1994-1998) and the passing on of Kim Il Sung, DPRK's eternal President, the Kim Jong Il regime was faced with unprecedented challenges that no leaders in the DPRK had experienced before. The advent of DPRK's nuclear program, alongside the belligerent narrative in highlighting the Japan, United States and South Korea as external threats were interpreted by analysts that this was done as a rallying cry for the North Korean people to stand resolutely behind the Kim regime regardless of the hardship involved. It was a misdirection to divert the North Korean people's attention from the troubles that DPRK faces, the mismanagement of the economy by the elites, and succession issue. Yet, with the DPRK test firing missiles that flew over Japan (DPRK billed this as a satellite launch), public opinion intensified against the DPRK. This prompted a more liberal discussion within Japan on how should relations with the North Koreans (and by extension) China be handled. During Prime Minister Koizumi's tenure, Japan's North Korean policy was principally under the purview of Chief Cabinet Secretary (then Shinzo Abe). Kim Jong Il's diplomatic naïveté (or recklessness) in admitting that North Korea was principally responsible for the kidnapping of Japanese nationals during the Cold War was a huge political coup for the Koizumi administration, and it brought about the repercussions beyond the imagination of the late DPRK leader. Kim Jong-Il had probably hoped that this admission would lead to political closure and better relations with Japan, but instead this backfired. Even though this admission gained Koizumi and Abe a lot of political credit, the incessant pressure exacted by public opinion and the endurance of this issue in Japanese domestic politics probably resulted in a political net loss for the administration. Over the last decade, Tokyo's position increasingly hardened, many officials are increasingly convinced that co-operation with her neighbors are impossible. How does Japan's evolving diplomacy deal with these challenges then?

JAPAN'S EVOLVING DIPLOMACY AND SINO-JAPANESE RELATIONS

In recent years, there appeared to be two primary strategies that Japan is undertaking to tackle the challenges aforementioned. The first has to do with the alliance Treaty Japan has with the United States. The Treaty of Mutual Co-operation and Security between United States and Japan was formerly established in 1951, revised in 1960, 1997 and several times afterwards.[30] The US-Japan security today is described as a grand bargain[31], and indeed the "bedrock" of the peace and stability in the Asia-Pacific Region", the "anchor of peace and stability" or that relationship that "underwrites the freedom and prosperity in the region". Even as the demise of the USSR meant that the principal threat that underpin the rationale for the alliance was gone, Japan saw it in their best interest to shore up and strengthen the US-Japan Security alliance—as a shield for Japan's gradual strengthening of the Japan Self Defense Force as well as a blanket of reassurance for Japan's neighbors with regards to Japan's plan. This would also placate the Americans who have been urging Japan to "do more" for the alliance, and provide suitable opportunities for Japan to play a global role.

Internally, Japan's principal debate and focus is on the postwar institutions that the center-of-right and right wing politicians have come to see as the bane of Japanese progressiveness. Specifically, the debate is centered upon Article 9 of the Constitution that removes Japan's sovereign right of war-making, and as well as the constraints the Constitution puts on Japan's ability to participate collective security. The Constitution in fact is a legal and political latch on Japan's strategic abilities and is the main instrument that gives the idea of Japanese pacifism any credibility. Beyond that, it is the Constitution that has often enabled the Japanese to downplay demands from her alliance partner to play a bigger role in global affairs. With the affirmation and revision of the US-Japan security Treaty in 1997, Tokyo has taken on incremental steps to remove legal impediments that allows for a more flexible and agile interpretation of the law that would facilitate Japan in assisting with US deployments[32] in contingencies affecting Japan even as the debate on the Constitution rages on.

With the possible exception of Prime Minister Hatoyama, most of the Post-Cold War Prime Ministers have been staunch supporters of the United States. In principle, regardless of whether they had a personal dislike (or not) for the US, the long "cherished" position is that Japan would remain the principal alliance partner of the United States in Asia-Pacific. This stems from a deep seeded affinity that the Liberal Democratic Party has with the United States since the LDP's inception in 1955. In recognition of U.S. role in East Asia and the support for the US-Japan alliance, the LDP in turn has always enjoyed U.S. patronage in Japan's political system. Japan had benefitted tremendously from this arrangement and most of the Prime Ministers saw no point in deviating from this. To this end, the US-Japan relations had always been one that reflected perfect asymmetry. Regardless of how this Treaty is being interpreted or propagated, US-Japan relations is never one between equal sovereigns. This façade is one of the principal reasons why US policymakers insist on keeping this alliance and why a manifestation of Japanese nationalism has always been its rhetoric against the United States (not just China or the Koreas). Yet regardless of this nationalistic grumbling within Japan, the United States have always been able to keep these sentiments in check—even when Japan was led by the Democratic Party of Japan—a party that came to power riding on voters dissatisfaction with the Liberal Democratic Party.

If we take a step back in the Japan strategic narratives in the post-Cold War world, what was being discussed in Japan during the 1990s corresponded quite similarly to the post September 11 strategic agenda in Asia. Japan is principally concerned with (1) the rise of China and (2) her relationship with the United States. By 2000, Tokyo was already working to on a series of legislation to strengthen the logistical side of the US-Japan Treaty. Prime Minister Koizumi's tenure—one of Japan's most popular Prime ministers in recent decades overlapped substantially with that of President George W. Bush. The era of Bush administration is likely to go down in history books as one of the most aggressive periods in US foreign policy—remembered for the War on Terror, the overthrow of the Saddam Regime in Iraq and the prosecution of two theatre operations in Afghanistan. Many countries in the Asia-Pacific regard that the United States had effectively neglected the region as the United States have focused on Iraq and Afghanistan, hence the need to "pivot" US diplomacy back to Asia when the Americans scaled down their involvement in the Middle East.[33] In fact, some scholars have attested that this period is one of the "golden" years of US-Japan relations. Japan appears to be doing more with "less" in terms of strengthening the alliance. Victor Cha observes that there is an unprecedented level of intimacy between the Japan and the United States.[34] Japan's diplomacy in fact took a big step forward through her deployments to both support logistical support (refueling) for the United States in the Indian Ocean and to participate the missions in the Gulf of Aden. Koizumi's aspiration with regards to the US-Japan alliance was to ensure that Japan becomes United States' "Great Britain" in Asia. The US-Japan alliance is therefore never tighter before.

Conversely, the "hands off" approach[35] and silence of the United States towards the confrontation between China and Japan throughout the Bush Administration contributed to deterioration of Sino-Japanese relations. From 2000 onwards, Japan's relationship with the United States grew from strength to strength—whilst Japan's relationship with China spiraled downwards, culminating in widespread protests in each and every city in the PRC by the end of Koizumi's tenure. Many analysts attributed the deterioration of Sino-Japanese relations to the United States—suggesting that the US had failed to ameliorate tensions between the two Asian giants either out of intentional policy or through neglect. However, the converse could be true: the US's Asia-Pacific under George Bush has been extremely successful. The Bush administration has been able to propel US-Japan relations to greater heights, and at the same time because of the fall out in Sino-Japanese relations—has caused the Chinese to move closer to the United States in order to secure their help to manage relations with Japan.

In turn, Japan however got precious little help from this staunch profession of friendship with the United States. The Americans never supported Japan's lobbying on the North Korean issue, especially with regards to the kidnapped Japanese nationals;[36] Japan's relations with China was at an all-time low, and despite repeated clarifications sought by Japanese officials, the ambivalent position that the United States took did not give Japanese officials the security comfort they were looking for in the sense that they would be sure that the United States would come to their aid if a Sino-Japanese confrontation occur. However, the LDP politicians primarily did benefit from the standoff with China and the DPRK during this period. LDP Prime Ministers from Koizumi to Abe had managed to rally the country around the DPRK kidnapping issue, dispatched ships to the Indian Ocean, sent a humanitarian contingent to Iraq, and upgraded the status of the defense ministry. All in, Japan's mainstream political spectrum has shifted rightwards, and any illusions that pacifism still pervades Japanese thinking needs to be reconsidered carefully.

RETHINKING JAPAN'S RELATIONS WITH THE UNITED STATES AND CHINA

Most International relations scholars only focuses on the relationship between the governments and relations between states, and neglect what goes on in the ground—i.e. the people-to-people relations. Mao Zedong and Chiang Kaishek were too keen to exclude each other in international diplomatic recognition and pursued "normalization" with the United States and Japan without much domestic consultation. What the Chinese people felt and thought then did not matter. Without addressing the difficulty issues head on, they let sentiments and anger simmer for over a generation. Although many American and Japanese Scholars suggest that these sentiments are results of a "top-down instrumental usage" by the Communist Party seeking greater legitimacy, most Chinese scholars would suggest that the real picture is a lot less simple and neater than this explanation suggests. If anything, they would say that the sentiments are genuinely felt.

Today, public opinion polls published in China and Japan tells us that Chinese people and Japanese people have increasingly negative views of each other. This might be true but aside from questioning the assumptions, methodology and sample size of these surveys, these polls tells us nothing definitive about Sino-Japanese relations. How can we be sure that the sample size of a few hundred people are representative of the entire Japanese or the Chinese nation? One might even ask if these "straw polls" affect Sino-Japanese relations—given the repeated emphasis on the negative in the mass media.

We often hear the phrases like Chinese and Japanese have increasingly different "values" etc.[37] This type of shallow assertion is not quite true. Japanese and Chinese people in fact share many similarities in values—and perhaps these similarities that cause them to try and assert their differences from each other. The identity politics we see today in Sino-Japanese relations is one such manifestation. Both Chinese, Japanese (and to a large extent the Koreans) are all very nationalistic (that in itself is a similarity) and most of these people are immensely proud of their culture and they all feel that their nation is the "greatest" country ever. We are told also that Japanese and Americans have many shared values—but is this really true? Japanese people like to go to the United States and Europe to experience the culture precisely because these cultures are so foreign. The truth about the "different values" debate between China and Japan is probably somewhat in between: the Chinese and Japanese probably share more in common than they assume, and the Americans and Japanese do not have all that much in commonality than they think they do. The problem is that because of the politics—Japanese and Chinese tend to assume the worst in each other than they really are.

Many countries and people around the world, especially those in Asia have a deep admiration[38] for Japan and her achievements in the past seven decades. Japan has given the world the first color TV and music Walkman. Ubiquitous Toyota and Nissan cars ply highways and streets from Bosnia to Malawi, from Beirut to Caracas. Year after year, millions of people visit and fell in love with Japan. No one can resist the charms of Tokyo in springtime or the allure of Kyoto in autumn. The beauty of Hokkaido in Summer and Akita's amazing Onsen in winter are just as unforgettable. Then there are those that are mesmerized by Japanese classical and popular culture. Even those people whom the Japanese think "hate" Japan are in reality major fans of things Japanese—from sushi to sumo. Japanese do not have to look far—just ask the ever increasing number of Chinese tourists flocking to Japan every year.[39]

But it is not just popular culture or technological products that people admire Japan for. People around the world also admire Japan for her Peace Constitution. Japan's Constitution and the extraordinary effort of Japan to uphold and promote the ideals of Peace since the end of the Second World

War have not escaped attention of most Asian countries. This institution is the most single source of Japan's soft power and legitimacy in world politics today. Unfortunately it is this particular institution that many popular Japanese politicians are seeking to erode.

While Prime Minister Kishi was instrumental in revising and pushing through the US-Japan Security Alliance, his grandson, Prime Minster Abe is aiming to loosen the Constitutional shackles to allow Japan to participate in Collective Security, and to allow the JSDF to have greater strategic latitude in the use of force.[40] Under the leadership of Prime Minister Abe, the Japan Defense Agency was upgraded to full Ministry status, and the Constitution reinterpreted. In particular Article 9 of Japan's constitution was reinterpreted to permit Japan to maintain de jure (in law) military forces. By the end of 2013, he advocated a major shift in Japan's defense posture in the name of "proactive pacifism" which saw a major expansion of Japan's defense capabilities.[41] To a limited extent, this is music to the United States: after all Washington has been encouraging Japan to do "more" for their own security, with a preference for a "stronger Japan in a stronger alliance". The politicians and bureaucrats suggest this is the right thing to do—in particular for Japan's normalization. With this policy orientation, Japan might put in more troops to the alliance, commit more and more suitable resources for basing arrangements, and forward more monetary and logistical resources to enhance US or US-Japan military operations. From the Koizumi administration onwards, there has been creeping legal revisionism in the form of directives, secondary legislation from the various ministries in order to loosen the constitutional grip.[42] Today, Japanese officials are convinced that this is the correct thing to do, but if normalization means obtaining more political leeway and freewill (ostensibly from the US), then this is going exactly the wrong way.

What does all this development mean for Sino-Japanese relations then? The primary precipitating driver of recent tensions with China appeared to revolve around the issue of the Senkaku/Diaoyu island. Even though this is primarily not of Abe's doing but precipitated from the then Tokyo governor, Shintaro Ishihara's attempt to buy the island and maneuver the DPJ administration into a corner,[43] the timing cannot be better for the Abe administration. The issue has enabled the center-of-right wing politicians to completely eradicate any sympathy residual that the Japanese people have for China. The root driver of these events still traces to the singular cause of the threat caused by China's rise and the implications it holds for the United States and Japan.

These are testing times not only for Japan but the rest of Asia. Regardless of the complexities of Sino-Japanese relations, these issues in Sino-Japanese relations are becoming interlinked and securitized. The real discomfort for many in Asia—is to watch from the sidelines as China and Japan appears to be locked in a hegemonic contestation. Regional countries do not want to be asked to take sides. Both Japan and China must understand this—if either country aspires to be acknowledged as a Great Power and profess ambition of regional leadership, then it must do its utmost to take into its sentiments of the countries that it professes to want to lead.

Even though the US-Japan alliance appears to unite the US and Japan on balancing China, Washington and Tokyo both have very different agendas with regards to East Asia. Beyond that, that is a major difference between what the United States can and want to achieve and what the Japanese can and want to achieve with regards to China.

For the United States, maintaining hegemony in the Western Pacific and East Asia is essential to the United States' status as the world's sole super-power and national interests. Currently, East Asia and Oceania spends USD$403 billion on advance weaponry, which is a significant percent in turns supports much of the R & D in the United States. East Asia accounts for about 25% of the world expenditure on weapons.[44] Japan and China accounts for more than 50% of US Treasury bonds, with China holding $1.3 Trillion and Japan holding $1.18 billion at the end of 2013.[45] The markets of China, Japan, South Korea, Taiwan and Southeast Asia provide markets for US exports, and these same emerging economies are enablers of the power of the US currency. The United States maintains that it takes a more dispassion-ate view towards quarrels in Sino-Japanese relations, and often has a non-prescription approach towards disputes in Sino-Japanese quarrels. It is im-portant to note that in a large part the demand for the United States' leader-ship, as well as her ability to influence events in Western Pacific has to do with her ability to cultivate asymmetric relations with China and Japan re-spectively. In other words, the ability to maintain extremely good relations with China and Japan and prevent China and Japan from valuing and ranking each other diplomatically and politically higher than they do with the United States underpin the US influence in the region.

For Japan, the China problem is a vexing one. Be that as it may, Japan's China problem is not a new one and has been around since Japan's early history. To be precise, from the 15th Century, China has been the number one obsession in Japanese elites minds. Conversely, the problem with the Chi-nese is that they have always disregarded Japan as inconsequential—in fact, this is probably one of the biggest failures of recent Chinese elites. Even today, seven decades after a century of protracted war –China and the Chi-nese are still making the same mistakes. For China, dealing with Japan is often viewed through the prism of dealing with the United States—as if Tokyo is inconsequential. This is inadequate and wrong.

For Tokyo, the question of containing China is now a mainstream policy debate, not a private coffee break conversation amongst politicians. The problem in Japan today is that rather than to work things out with China, many feels it necessary to involve the United States because of the US's experience and clout in strategic matters. Tokyo's approach with Beijing (and vice-versa) thus is increasing rigid, with little room for maneuverability. There have been no politicians of stature and vision in this set of bilateral relations that can ameliorate the hostilities. All the broad-brushed diplomatic principles[46] that the previous generation of Chinese and Japanese leaders that had guided Japan and China so delicately throughout the Cold War are gone. Japan's antagonism with China has taken on a life of its own and bilateral relations now appear overtly focused on minute matters and tit-for-tat maneuvers. Track II activities since 2005 has decreased and would continue to do. Even as many Japanese scholars might disagree: Japan does not gain (neither does China) through the maintenance of a tense Sino-Japanese Relations. This chapter considers that it is important not to attribute blame (or who is responsible for what) for the decline of relationship, but really to consider what could be done to further this bilateral relationship.

BRING THE FUNDAMENTALS OF JAPANESE FOREIGN POLICY TO THE FORE

As Japan stops and reconsiders her future direction in foreign affairs after the Cold War and the War on Terror—it is important to consider many of the arguments that are put forth. One salient school of thought calls for the modification of the Japanese Constitution in part or whole. These revisionists often argue that it is important for the Japanese people to remember that although the Constitution was "forced" upon Japan. This is only partially true, as a number of people in the Japanese government at that time were involved in the drafting, not just the planners from General MacArthur's stuff. At the same time, it was also protected and honored by an entire generation of Japanese. People might not believe it, but not soon after General MacArthur and his team "imposed" the Constitution on Japan, American strategic planners realized what a major mistake they have made. With the onset of the Cold War, they tried their best to have the Constitution revised (or undermined). The Japanese people was not sympathetic. In 1951, the Americans once again imposed the US-Japan Treaty—and this was again did not receive a warm reception either. In fact, the Treaty totally disregarded the spirit of the Peace Constitution, but the Japanese government was able to justify it by supersizing the Communist threat. One needs not look far for evidence, Prime Minister Kishi found himself under extraordinary amount of pressure when he tried to force through the US-Japan Security Treaty through the Diet. Massive riots broke in May and June 1960 out on the steps of the Japanese Diet after the Treaty was ratified.[47] Today, Prime Minister Abe's political platform seems to be aimed at achieving what his grandfather was not able to do, but today's Japan is a far more tolerant one than the one his grandfather's generation day for his agenda.

Prime Minister Abe is not very popular in China or in Korea for obvious reasons. For someone who is extremely vocal on making a "new and beautiful" Japan—outside of Japan, he is one that appears to be embodied by aspirations of the past. He is popular in Japan—seen as a strong leader and embodiment of hope and inspiration for the post War generation. It is understandable why this generation would feel this way. This is a generation that was born after the Second World War and grew up in a Japan that became the second largest economy in the World (just like the Chinese today). They have never experienced War and defeat, occupation and despondence (much can be said for the Chinese who never experienced war and did live through the upheaval of Great Leap Forward and Cultural Revolution). The current generation of Japanese leaders grew up in a Japan that became an economic superpower in the 1980s, and whose "normal" foreign relations is one Japan has a strong alliance with United States.

Viewed from outside Japan, the Japanese Constitution is considered by many to be one of the finest postwar institutions ever built. Even though there is a segment of people (and politicians) who view Article 9 of the Constitution as a "constraint" on Japan realpolitik interests, and responsible for the erosion of the fighting spirit of younger Japanese, the flip side of this perception outside has not be discussed adequately within Japan. Article 9 outside of Japan carries different meanings to different people, for many in and outside of Japan.

The Peace constitution is one of the firmest manifestations of Japan's resolve to pacifism. Even more so, it is testament of Japan's apology to the world. There is a difference in not having sovereign right to war at all, and having that right and maintaining a position that renouncing the right. Japan has made a conscious choice to renounce that right for over six decades. To that end, removing Article 9 might mean removing the apology to the nations hurt during the war. That may actually be more problematic in the long run even though it looks like a strategically viable option today. In doing so, it removes any residual goodwill in China and Korea. Beyond that, the Constitution could also be seen as a security guarantee to the Chinese, Koreans and surprisingly the Japanese themselves—even though this has never been discussed explicitly. Abe's actions have also gravely caused concerns in China and the Koreas. Chinese President Xi Jinping's July 2014 visit to South Korea is both a signal to the DPRK just it is to the Japan and the United States of China's evolving defense posture.

The utility for Japan's continued embrace of the US-Japan Security Treaty is a more sophisticated question. Japan's embrace of the United States might actually have more to do with the question of "abandonment" than anything else. There is now an idea that the United States and China should form some sort of alliance between them to resolve many of the major problems in the world—and to that extent this idea has been given the name of a G2. [48] Hugh White of Australia National University argues that China and the United States should consider "sharing" power, not that China is better than other countries, or that the United States should "give way" to the rising hegemon, but rather with China on board, a lot of global problems could be solved. Other scholars have articulated similar arguments that the United States might find a more "natural" partner in China than in Japan— again this is premised on the fact that China is often the source of the problems (e.g. infectious diseases, organized crime). Perhaps this is why Tokyo is often so nervous about the prospects of this materializing. If and when the United States move to cement a strong alliance with China, Tokyo is probably worried that her prospects in playing a leadership role with the US backing in Asia would be eroded.

However, it is important to remember this: despite the rhetoric, the United States make foreign policy to enhance US national interests, not Japanese interests. Even though Washington argues that it does, the priority is to ensure US interests prevail. Japan's interests cannot be guaranteed by the US-Japan alliance alone, and Tokyo knows this as well as anyone. In the long run, Japan should aspire to see if there are ways to move ahead and work with China too. In fact, Prime Minister Abe with his nationalistic credentials may be in the best position to forge strong relations with China, as no one would be able to accuse him of "selling" out the country's interests. A candidate with a lesser nationalistic political capital might not be able to do this. Japan surely realizes that even if Japan shoulders more responsibility for her own defense needs through her normalization, the ultimate test is if Japan have more independent and autonomous control of the JSDF and other territory.

Beyond that, would the United States be prepared to involve Japan in more responsibilities in other regions such as the Middle East or South Asia? Even with the recent revision signifying that the scope of the Treaty has been globalised, it is not entirely clear that if Japan's status has been upgraded from a junior partner status to something more substantial—even if the Washington has spared no effort to accord Japanese Prime Minister Abe with all trappings of a full State visit and an address to the United States Congress. [49] Here the real question would be: would the US allow Japan a bigger and more special position in global affairs, say nuclear negotiations involving Iran or say the Arab-Israeli dispute for instance? Japan's normalization should come about not only in military terms (to contain China or the DPRK) but also politically (to become more autonomous of U.S. influence). This remains to be seen.

Insofar when Sino-Japanese relations are concerned, it is important issues both nations are encouraged to frame issues in a non-zero-sum manner. This is easier said than done, but China and Japan elites could consider the following: First, if China and Japan cannot co-operate strategically in Asia-Pacific, there are enough problems outside the region that both China and Japan can work on. For instance, the provision of international public goods—like the joint naval task force to tackle the piracy problems or the perhaps in helping bring pipe water to isolated parts of Africa and Latin America or co-sponsoring poverty alleviation or health projects might be a way out to build more confidence. Instead of focusing their energy on competitive strategies to fight for territorial possessions or resources in the East China Sea, these projects could actually be good for Sino-Japanese relations can lay the basis for Sino-Japanese relations in the long run.

Second, both nations should recognize that security competition would only impoverish both nations, and they would be better off diverting the resources to more needed domestic uses. Both countries have a greying population, and money spent on massive militarization to "defend" the islands could be diverted to healthcare or social security etc. The only parties winning in any arms race are the arms manufacturers, and unless China and Japan are becoming keen to export arms for political reasons, spending excessively on defence needs would not be wise. If we confine the discussion to the territorial issues, both nations should recognize that Senkaku/Diaoyu Islands was a non-issue for many years, but only resurfaced after Japan's attempt to buy the islands. Both nations should recognize that the only way the issue could become less contentious is for both the government and the media in particular to shift the focus away from it, allowing the issue to slowly subside away from the limelight.

Today, the United States and Japan are getting anxious about China's strategic rise, pointing to the opaque budget of the PLA and the military modernization that is underway in China. Through political, diplomatic and strategic measures, both countries are doing their best to "balance" this rise. China in turn perceives this as "containment", and enacts various measures to circumvent the maneuvers of the US and Japan. A vicious cycle thus surely ensues. This was hardly an issue during the Cold War, as the United States and Japan maintained a wide "gap" between their capabilities and China's, which is now diminishing far more quickly than what Washington and Tokyo can hope for. This then begs the question: what kind of "gap" should exist between the Chinese, the Americans and the Japanese that would be "comfortable" for all three powers to live in harmony? The answer is none, because if we are to frame issues in these terms—military competition would inevitable. What is important is here is that that all three nations should acknowledge that they and the others have valid security concerns. Asking each other to give up on their "interests" or "concerns" is not just going to work. With an eye on the future, there is no guarantee that China's rise will definitely be a security challenge to Japan. What is certain however is that if one treats China like an enemy, it would become a self-fulfilling prophecy.

It is important that both nations do not avoid the problems caused by the rift—as the longer it simmers, the less likely the two nations will ever see eye to eye and have a frank discussion. At the time of writing, one of the most important things that the two nations could do is to compartmentalize the dispute and prevent the issues from being linked to each other—even if public opinion does. The essentially prevents issues from becoming protracted and limits the securitization process of these bilateral issues. Mel Gurtov [50] has highlighted a series of steps that can be implemented at Track I, II, and III levels: (1) regularization of high-level diplomacy; (2) mutual appreciation; (3) Affirmations of Good intentions; (4) Creating a Northeast Asia Security Dialogue mechanisms (5) having the US play the peacemaker role between China and Japan and declare unambiguously its opposition to worsening Sino-Japanese relations. There would be varying views to the effectiveness and efficacy of these measures.

At this juncture, one positive step that the Chinese and Japanese could do is for both nations to at least recognize each other's contributions to the global order. It is particularly important that if the politicians cannot do this, then it is up to journalists, scholars and other non-government institutions that make and lead public opinion take on this role. Professors, researchers, journalists and writers—the bulwark of civil society should be careful in repeating government rhetoric as they have a responsibility to educate the next generation and contribute to public well-being. If the civil society in both China and Japan can take the lead in combating bigotry and falsehood, and disallow political agendas to drive bilateral relations, it is not inconceivable that China and Japan can take a big step forward. Since politicians appears (or at least profess) to "follow" public opinion, and if public opinion indeed calls for better relations, it would put the onus for the politicians to act more appropriately when dealing with bilateral issues.

As the author has argued frequently, there are many things that China can learn from Japan and Japanese nation. For instance, the concept of humility, the spirit of excellence and nation-before-self mentality of the Japanese people that is so lacking in China and critical for Chinese modernization. As for Japan, the author is of the view that the Japanese people would be wise enough to ensure that the country stay on course to ensure the Peace in East Asia, as they have done over the last few decades. Indeed the Japanese nation should also be far-sighted enough to discuss and debate the kind of relations they want with China and East Asia over the years to come. At the end of the day, Japanese people must ask this question: would hyping up the China and North Korean threat, shoring up the military alliance and amending the Constitution actually bring them greater security? Likewise, the Chinese nation should better reflect on how they could better express their grievance in a more positive way. East Asia can only become harmonious if and only if China and Japan can consider the stakes more carefully, and that civil society as opposed to politicians in both countries lead the way to find common ground that has been so badly eroded over the last two decades.

NOTES

1. The author gratefully acknowledges the support of the Hong Kong Research Council General Research Fund for its support for the project entitled "The Prospects and Challenges of Japan's Normalization: A Case Study of Japanese Diplomatic and Security Activities in the Middle East from 1991-2009" (Project Number 753310) for which the chapter draws its parts of its findings from. The author would also like to thank the Professor Yoneyuki Sugita and other colleagues for the comments on earlier draft versions of this chapter. Needless to say, the errors contained therein are the author's sole responsibility.

2. Hiroko Tabuchi, "Japan Scambles Jet in Island Dispute with China," *The New York Times*, 13 December 2012, last accessed 10 June 2015, http://www.nytimes.com/2012/12/14/world/asia/japan-scrambles-jets-in-island-dispute-with-china.html?_r=0 ; also see "Japan seeks her own early warning aircraft," *South China Morning Post*, 22 September 2014, last accessed 10 June 2015, http://www.scmp.com/news/asia/article/1597600/japan-seeks-its-own-early-warning-aircraft ; Isabel Reynolds and Takashi Hirokawa, "Abe Warns China on Island Spat as Japan Dispatches Jets," 28 Oct 2013, *Bloomberg*, last accessed 10 June 2015, http://www.bloomberg.com/news/2013-10-28/abe-warns-china-on-island-spat-as-japan-dispatches-fighter-jets.html

3. Kathrin Hille, "Chinese Navy on Exercise Near Senkakus," *Financial Times*, 19 October 2012, last accessed 10 June 2015, http://www.ft.com/intl/cms/s/0/0eb9e91a-19be-11e2-a379-00144feabdc0.html#axzz3EXNxpLsS ; Kyle Mizokami, "How China sparked an Asian frenzy for killer submarines," *The Week* editorial, 29 August 2014, last accessed 10 June 2015, http://theweek.com/article/index/266754/how-china-sparked-an-asian-frenzy-for-killer-submarines

4. "日媒稱日本無力應對中方巡航釣魚島," (Japanese Media Says Japan has no ability to defence Diaoyu islands) *Sina News*, 10 September 2014, last accessed 10 June 2015, http://news.sina.com.hk/news/20140910/-12-3357204/1.html

5. Ben McLannahan and Geoff Dyer, "US urge restraint in Senkaku Dispute," *Financial Times*, 17 September 2012, last accessed 10 June 2015, http://www.ft.com/intl/cms/s/0/0219cb88-0093-11e2-8197-00144feabdc0.html#axzz3EXNxpLsS

6. "Panetta tells China that Senkakus under the Japan-US Security Treaty", *The Asahi Shimbun*, 21 September 2012, last accessed 10 June 2015, http://ajw.asahi.com/article/asia/china/AJ201209210061 "Obama Asia Tour: US-Japan Treaty "covers disputed islands," *BBC News*, 24 April 2014, last accessed 10 June 2015, http://www.bbc.com/news/world-asia-27137272 ; also see Tstsuo Kotani, "The Senkaku Islands and the US-Japan Alliance: Future Implications for the Asia-Pacific," Project 2049 Paper, last accessed 10 June 2015, http://project2049.net/documents/senkaku_kotani.pdf

7. It would be impossible for any academic from the top tier national institutions in either China or Japan (or for that matter the Koreas) to be able to take a position that differ radically from their governments due to the fact that their positions are often "civil service" positions. These positions often carry with them corresponding expectations of behavior and attitudes towards certain issues. Furthermore, even though they might privately feel sympathetic and see the logic behind the "other's claims, they would probably be unable to acquiesce or agree such sentiments publicly.

8. The identification of China as an explicit threat, see "China criticizes warnings in Japan's defense white paper as groundless," *The Japan Times*, 5 August 2014, last accessed 10 June 2015, http://www.japantimes.co.jp/news/2014/08/05/national/politics-diplomacy/china-criticizes-warnings-in-japans-defense-white-paper-as-groundless/#.VCdqAP06_T4 ; also see "China media: Japan defense paper", *BBC News China*, 6 August 2014, last accessed 10 June 2015, http://www.bbc.com/news/world-asia-china-28671227

9. In a recent poll by Genron and China daily, 53.4% of Chinese survey envisaged a future conflict with Japan, whilst 29% of Japanese say they expected a loom military conflict. 93% of Japanese respondents said their impression of China was "unfavorable" worsening from 90.1% in last year and this is the highest level since 2005. See "53pc of Chinese expect to go to war with Japan: poll," *South China Morning Post*, 10 September 2014, last accessed 10 June 2015, http://www.scmp.com/news/asia/article/1589311/more-half-chinese-anticipate-war-japan-survey?page=all

10. The statistics here are derived from OECD.website: "OECD Better Life Index," OECD, last accessed 10 June 2015, http://www.oecdbetterlifeindex.org/countries/; South Korea's average is USD$18,035, whereas in the United States it is USD$39,531.

11. "Economic and Social Commission for East Asia," in *Statistical Year Book for Asia and Pacific 2013*, USCAP United Nations, last accessed 10 June 2015, http://www.unescap.org/resources/statistical-yearbook-asia-and-pacific-2013

12. Lynann Butkiewicz, "The Implications of Japan's Changing Demographics," The National Bureau of Asian Research Report, last accessed 10 June 2015, http://www.nbr.org/downloads/pdfs/ETA/ES_Japan_demographics_report.pdf

13. Milton Eszrati, "Japan's Aging Economics." *Foreign Affairs*, 1 May 1997, last accessed 10 June 2015, http://www.foreignaffairs.com/articles/53050/milton-ezrati/japans-aging-economics

14. Sawako Obara, "Abuse of Elderly Up, Often Unintended," *The Japan Times*, 30 January 2010, last accessed 10 June 2015, http://www.japantimes.co.jp/news/2010/01/30/national/abuse-of-elderly-up-said-often-unintended/#.U7Xa4xYijwI

15. Figures from Japan's National Institute of Population and Social Security Research, last accessed 10 June 2015, http://www.ipss.go.jp/site-ad/TopPageData/Pyramid_a.html

16. Eleanor Warnock, "Japan's Aging reflects Asia's Future," *The Wall Street Journal Japan*, 6 January 2014, last accessed 10 June 2015, http://blogs.wsj.com/japanrealtime/2014/01/06/japans-aging-reflects-asias-future/

17. Masaaki Kanno, "The Problems with Japan's economic experiment," *Financial Times*, 3 February 2013, last accessed 10 June 2015, http://www.ft.com/cms/s/0/4a4aacee-6bbc-11e2-a700-00144feab49a.html#axzz36RXkGo5e

18. The current Prime Minister Shinzo Abe is more of a foreign and security Prime Minister than anyone of his predecessors – including the political maverick Prime Minister Junichiro Koizumi.

19. Notwithstanding the economic and financial challenges, today Japan too faces a host of foreign policy problems that their colleagues in the 1970s and 1980s never had to deal with. In the early years after the war, after the merger of the Liberal and Democratic Party, Japan was primarily faced with the crisis of revamping the US-Japan security alliance. It took the LDP, under the leadership of Prime Minister Nobusuke Kishi who pushed through the bill to effect the revised US-Japan Security Treaty. That event was possibly the only event in Japan's post War history to be so riled with emotion and so contested – at least this was the case until the current revision of the Constitution.

20. Nakanishi Hiroshi, "The Gulf War and Japanese Diplomacy," *Nippon*, 6 December 2011, last accessed 10 June 2015, http://www.nippon.com/en/features/c00202/

21. "China's Nuclear Ambition Grows", *The Risk Report*, Volume 1 Number 9 (November 1995), last accessed 10 June 2015, http://www.wisconsinproject.org/countries/china/nuc-amb.html

22. "Nations condemn Chinese missile tests," *CNN News*, 8 March 1996, last accessed 10 June 2015, http://edition.cnn.com/WORLD/9603/china_taiwan/08/

23. "New Regime for Security Alliance," *The Japan Times*, 28 April 2015, last accessed 10 June 2015, http://www.japantimes.co.jp/opinion/2015/04/28/editorials/new-regime-for-security-alliance/#.VXhTFWAdIZM

24. "Japan refuses China clear-cut apology," *BBC News*, 26 November 1998, last accessed 10 June 2015, http://news.bbc.co.uk/2/hi/asia-pacific/222328.stm

25. "Japan Coast Guard Fires at Fishing Boat," *CNN News*, 22 December 2001, last accessed 10 June 2015, http://edition.cnn.com/2001/WORLD/asiapcf/east/12/22/japan.suspiciousboat/index.html

26. "China vs. Japan: A Phony trade War," *Bloomberg*, 8 July 2001, last accessed 10 June 2015, http://www.bloomberg.com/bw/stories/2001-07-08/china-vs-dot-japan-a-phony-trade-war

27. "How uninhabited islands soured China-Japan ties", *BBC News*, 10 November 2014, last accessed 10 June 2015, http://www.bbc.com/news/world-asia-pacific-11341139

28. Refers to the Japan's Prime Minister's Office, see: "Prime Minister of Japan and His Cabinet," Cabinet Public Relations Office, last accessed 10 June 2015, http://www.kantei.go.jp

29. The White Papers are published by the Ministry of Defense annually, and copies are available online: "Defense of Japan (multiple years)," Japan Ministry of Defense, last accessed 10 June 2015, http://www.mod.go.jp/e/publ/w_paper/

30. For more details, see the developments of the Japan-U.S. Security Consultative Committee (2+2 Meeting) from 2000 to 2014, available at Japan's Ministry of Foreign Affairs website: "Japan-U.S. Security Consultative Committee (2+2 Meeting)," Ministry of Foreign Affairs of Japan, last accessed 10 June 2015, http://www.mofa.go.jp/region/n-america/us/security/scc/index.html

31. George Packard, "The United States-Japan Security Treaty at 50: Still a Grand Bargain?" *Foreign Affairs*, March/ April 2010 Issue, last accessed 10 June 2015, http://www.foreignaffairs.com/articles/66150/george-r-packard/the-united-states-japan-security-treaty-at-50; For a copy of the Treaty (updated 2011) see the U.S. State Department website: "Agreement Between The United States of America and Japan Concerning New Special Measures Relating to Article XXIV of the Agreement Under Article VI of the Treaty of Mutual Cooperation and Security Between The United States of America and Japan, Regarding Facilities and Areas and the Status of United States Armed Forces in Japan," U.S. State Department, last accessed 10 June 2015, http://www.state.gov/documents/organization/163490.pdf

32. For example, see the US-Japan consultations over Security and Defense on Ballistic Missile Defense, Space, Cyberspace, Informational Security and Trilateral Cooperation: "The Japan-U.S. security Arrangements," Ministry of Foreign Affairs of Japan, last accessed 10 June 2015, http://www.mofa.go.jp/region/n-america/us/security/arrange.html

33. Greg Torode, "US is back in Asia, says Clinton," *South China Morning Post*, 23 July 2009, last accessed 10 June 2015, http://www.scmp.com/article/687604/us-back-asia-says-clinton

34. Victor Cha, "Winning Asia: Washington's Untold Success Story," *Foreign Affairs*, Nov/ Dec 2007 issue, last accessed 10 June 2015, http://www.foreignaffairs.com/articles/58454/victor-d-cha/winning-asia

35. Michael Wesley, "The dog that didn't bark: Bush and East Asian Regionalism" in *Bush and Asia: America's evolving relations with East Asia*, ed. Mark Beeson, (New York and Oxford: Routledge, 2003), 64-79; also see Victor Cha, "Winning Asia: Washington's Untold Success Story," *Foreign Affairs*, Nov/Dec 2007 issue, last accessed 10 June 2015, http://www.foreignaffairs.com/articles/58454/victor-d-cha/winning-asia; "China wins as US neglects region", *The Australian*, 3 September 2007, last accessed 10 June 2015, http://www.theaustralian.com.au/archive/news/china-wins-as-us-neglects-region/story-e6frg6sx-111114327058?nk=d13f46211119ba2ade5e3f2fd1f38524 ; "Hilary Clinton Declares US is back in Asia", *The China Post*, 22 July 2009, last accessed 10 June 2015, http://www.chinapost.com.tw/asia/regional-news/2009/07/22/217346/Hillary-Clinton.htm

36. "Japanese Officials Begin Abduction Talks in Pyongyang," *BBC news*, 28 October 2014, last accessed 10 June 2015, http://www.bbc.com/news/world-asia-29783103

37. "So Hard to be Friends," *The Economist*, 23 March 2005, last accessed 10 June 2015, http://www.economist.com/node/3786409

38. Roger Pulvers, "Will Japan's 'Positive Influence' Persist as it didn't before?" *The Japan Times*, 21 May 2006, last accessed 10 June 2015, http://www.japantimes.co.jp/opinion/2006/05/21/commentary/will-japans-positive-influence-persist-as-it-didnt-before/#.VXhZuGAdIZM

39. Adam Minter, "Why Chinese Tourists Love Japan," *Bloombergview*, 25 March 2015, last accessed 10 June 2015, http://www.bloombergview.com/articles/2015-03-25/why-chinese-tourists-love-japan

40. "Editorial – Japan's Security: Clear and Present Dangers" *Economist*, 5 July 2014, last accessed 10 June 2015, http://www.economist.com/news/asia/21606334-prime-minister-moves-japan-step-away-its-post-war-pacifism-clear-and-present-dangers

41. "Major Security Shift: Abe's proactive pacifism an exercise in military power in diplomacy," *Asahi Shimbun*, 14 July 2014, last accessed 10 June 2015, http://ajw.asahi.com/article/behind_news/politics/AJ201407140029

42. See MOFA's series of documents on the legislative and policy steps taken to enhance Japan's policies: "Japan's Security Policy," Ministry of Foreign Affairs of Japan, last accessed 10 June 2015, http://www.mofa.go.jp/policy/security/index.html

43. "Tokyo's Rightwing Governor Plans to Buy Disputed Senkaku Islands," *The Guardian*, 19 April 2012, last accessed 10 June 2015, http://www.theguardian.com/world/2012/apr/19/tokyo-governor-senkaku-islands-china

44. "Asia is world leader in expenditure on weapons in 2013," *Russian Radio*, 14 April 2014, last accessed 10 June 2015, http://indian.ruvr.ru/2014_04_14/Asia-is-the-world-leader-in-expenditure-on-weapons-in-2013-6784/

45. "China, Japan to boost US bonds buying to record high," *The Wall Street Journal*, 16 January 2014, last accessed 10 June 2015, http://online.wsj.com/news/articles/SB10001424052702304149404579324592538533768

46. For example, Deng's maxim to leave the solution of difficult problem like that of the Diaoyu/Senkaku island to the next generation.

47. Justin Jesty, "Tokyo 1960, Days of Rage and Grief: Hamaya Hiroshi's Photos of Anti-Security Treaty Protests," Massachusetts Institute of Technology Visualing Cultures, last accessed 10 June 2015, http://ocw.mit.edu/ans7870/21f/21f.027/tokyo_1960/anp2_essay01.html

48. The term was first coined by C. Fred Bergsten, *The United States and the World Economy,* (Washington DC: Institute of Economics Press, 2005); Also see Zbigniew Brzezinski, "The Group of Two that will Change the World," *Financial Times*, 13 January 2009, last accessed 10 June 2015, http://www.ft.com/intl/cms/s/0/d99369b8-e178-11dd-afa0-0000779fd2ac.html#axzz373oUx6Je; Also see Geoffrey Garrett, "China, the World and G2 in the G20 after the Global Financial Crisis," Global Policy, last accessed 10 June 2015, http://www.globalpolicyjournal.com/articles/world-economy-trade-and-finance/g2-g-20-china-united-states-and-world-after-global-financia; Also See Richard C. Bush III, "The United States and China: A G2 in the Making," *Brookings*, 11 October 2011, last accessed 10 June 2015, http://www.brookings.edu/research/articles/2011/10/11-china-us-g2-bush

49. See Speech by Shinzo Abe, "Toward an Alliance of Hope", Address to a Joint Meeting of the U.S. Congress by Prime Minister Shinzo Abe, 29 April 2015, http://japan.kantei.go.jp/97_abe/statement/201504/uscongress.html

50. Mel Gurtov, "Reconciling Japan and China," *The Asia-Pacific Journal: Japan Focus*, last accessed 10 June 2015, http://www.japanfocus.org/-Mel-Gurtov/2627/article.html

Chapter Four

Approaches to Resolving the Disputes in the East China Sea

Reinhard Drifte, Emeritus Professor,
University of Newcastle

The security situation of the East China Sea is dangerous and volatile and directly concerns all three bordering countries and impacts the regional role of the US as well as the trade interests of many countries: The Japanese-Chinese dispute about the title to some rocky islands between Taiwan and Okinawa in the East China Sea (ECS), called Senkaku Islands in Japanese and Diaoyu Islands in Chinese, is continuing since the latest major eruptions in 2010 and in 2012. Meanwhile, the demarcation of the EEZ (Exclusive Economic Zone) between all three states bordering the ECS—Japan, China and South Korea—is still pending. The absence of an agreed EEZ border between China and South Korea has led to a number of clashes between Chinese fishermen and South Korean coast guards which has cost lives on both sides. Tension between China and South Korea is also caused by the latter's incorporation of a submerged feature (Ieodo in Korean and Suyan rock in Chinese) which both sides claim to be within their EEZ. The rock is occupied by a South Korean ocean research station but China conducts patrols around it.[1] This dangerous situation as well as China's increasing challenges to the US regional dominance also influences the current and future role of the US in East Asia because of its alliance with Japan and South Korea.

The escalation of tensions is particularly visible from the territorial conflict around the Senkaku/Diaoyu Islands: The 2010 incident ended quickly with Japan's release of the captain. One reason for this is the fact that China's demand in 2010 was relatively clear and achievable (release of the captain) if painful for Japan at a time when it had a weak and inexperienced govern-

ment. But the crisis arising from China's strong reaction to the Japanese
government's purchase of three of the islands from their original private
owner in September 2012 caused Tokyo in turn to react intransigently because of the 2010 experience as well as other unfavourable domestic circumstances. The government was then replaced by the more hawkish Abe
government. The latter made the situation worse by a combination of continuing to deny the very existence of a territorial problem, a strengthening of
Japan's defence posture with explicit reference to the "China threat," and
statements and actions regarding certain contested aspects of Japan's pre-
1945 aggression against Asia. China has been reacting since then with a kind
of rhetorical warfare against Japan's alleged militarization and denial of what
China considers the correct narrative of history since the Sino-Japanese war
in 1894-5.

The most dangerous development since the 2012 crisis is the constant
confrontation between the navy and air forces of both Japan and China
around the disputed islands which led to several aerial near misses and the
rise in scramble activities by the Japanese air force. Tensions further increased, particularly since China established in November 2013 its own Air
Defence Identification Zone (ADIZ) which explicitly includes the air space
above the Senkaku/Diaoyu Islands, but also overlaps the South Korean ADIZ
and in particular encompasses the airspace above the Ieodo/Suyan rock. As a
result Seoul widened its ADIZ to include the rock. Moreover the Chinese
Navy is increasingly passing through international waters in the region and
accessing the Western Pacific from the East China Sea through the Japanese
archipelago. Neither Japan nor the US accept the Chinese ADIZ requirements (although in contrast to Japan, the US allows American civilian air-
lines to follow Chinese instructions to inform Chinese authorities before
entering the ADIZ) despite ominous Chinese warnings and several dangerous
close encounters. All the while the Chinese Coast Guard has established an
almost regular pattern of entering the Territorial Water, the Contiguous Zone
and the EEZ of the Senkaku/Diaoyu Islands despite Japan's Coast Guard
warning them about such intrusions. Fortunately so far the Japanese side has
left it to oral warnings and the frequency of the intrusions into the Territorial
Waters of the disputed islands has diminished.[2] These intrusions have continued after the 7 November 2014 statements by both sides although they have
at least led to a resumption of high-level talks and negotiations intended to
result in maritime and aerial communications mechanisms to be analysed
further down.

The security situation in the East China Sea continues therefore to be very
volatile and warrants serious considerations of means to ease the confrontation. Shi Yinhong, a professor at Renmin University in Beijing, predicts that
the conflict in the East China Sea as well as in the South China Sea will
intensify because of popular nationalism, dynamics within the Chinese

armed forces and because of the personal beliefs and strategic personalities of Beijing's top leaders.[3] Pei Minxin wrote that "At some point, the law of probability dictates that one of such incidents will lead to an actual conflict— either a mid-air or a maritime collision.[4]

But apart from the danger of a Japanese-Chinese military clash and the possible intervention of US forces under Article 5 of the mutual Japan-US Security Treaty, the confrontation over the Senkaku/Diaoyu Islands causes constant tensions between Japan and China, thus preventing the demarcation of the bilateral sea border which at least in the Southern part of the ECS can only be achieved once the territorial issue is solved. Furthermore, these tensions deprive both sides from exploiting their existing economic synergy (e.g. extracting oil and gas in the ECS, expanding trade and foreign direct investments), complicate the relationship between Japan and Korea and the US and China, and throw a dark shadow over the possibility of solving peacefully the territorial dispute between China and the other claimants in the South China Sea. The EEZ border demarcation conflict between China and South Korea is poisoning the bilateral relationship despite Seoul's attempt to play down the past clashes. From an even broader perspective, the various disputes in the East China Sea complicate the formation of a new regional order of which China and the US will be the major actors, and challenges international norms and legal order, such as the conduct of non-coercive diplomacy and the inviolability of international borders and sovereignty.

This chapter concentrates on the disputes between Japan and China in the ECS and proposes a step-by-step approach which at the end also considers several options to address the most difficult issue, i.e. the sovereignty issue of the Senkaku/Diaoyu Islands. The most neutral and effective way to resolve all disputes between all three countries would be international arbitration, i.e. the International Court of Justice (ICJ) for the territorial problem of the Senkaku/Diaoyu Islands, and the dispute settlement procedures of the United Nations Convention of the Law of the Sea (UNCLOS) for the Japan-China-South Korea EEZ border demarcation, but China has categorically refused any such arbitration. The Japanese government would be willing to accept the ICJ for the territorial conflict, but only if China brings the case to the Court lest it be perceived as acknowledging the existence of a territorial dispute.[5] Interestingly, a poll done in 2013 in several major Chinese cities found that there was a solid majority among the Chinese public for UN arbitration.[6] Japan did informally propose to China international arbitration of the EEZ issue but China declined.[7] South Korea has also ruled out compulsory dispute settlement for the delimitation of sea borders.[8] The only way forward is therefore bilateral negotiations on which this chapter focuses. China has always insisted on bilateral negotiations between the concerned countries (the same for the South China Sea disputes which it has with all bordering countries), but it has so far not clarified how to deal with the Northern part of the ECS where overlapping border claims require a Japan-South Korea-PRC negotiation process. Excluded from discussion here is the proposal by Taiwan's President Ma Yingjiu in 2012 for joint development of resources in the East China Sea (i.e. setting aside the islands dispute) because neither Japan nor the PRC would want to involve Taiwan.[9]

DOES ECONOMIC INTERDEPENDENCE EASE SECURITY CONFLICTS?

The urgency of measures to deal with the tensions in the ECS is not diminished by presumed benefits of economic interdependence. It is tempting to dismiss concerns about the tense security situation because the escalation of tensions has not yet led to a military clash which is at least partly attributed to the economic interdependence between all three countries. According to the Liberal School of International Relations theory, economic interdependence has a positive effect on the security dilemma. However, the absence so far of a clash does not mean that it cannot happen as some close encounters between the military of Japan and China since 2012 have shown. The "Cold Politics, Hot Economics" dichotomy during the Koizumi cabinet (2001-2006) turned out to be unsustainable since the Japan-China relationship still deteriorated despite a temporary improvement under the succeeding cabinets, leading finally to the 2010 and 2012 crises and today's tense security situation.

Moreover, the positive impact of economic interdependence between Japan and China has been diminished by the changes in the economic interdependence, and even more so by the diametrically opposed perceptions of this interdependence in both countries. For China, Japan's economic importance has been decreasing in relative terms (e.g. Japan occupying a smaller share of China's expanding overall trade with the world and China receiving less Japanese investment). This development and the expansion of China's economy certainly has had a negative influence on the Chinese government and the Chinese public during the 2010 and even more so during the 2012: the government imposed economic sanctions on Japan and Japanese businesses in China suffered from attacks and consumer boycotts. China in this way leveraged its supposedly stronger economic position to achieve victory in a sensitive area like territorial integrity.[10] As a result Japanese investment in China in 2014 fell by 38 % from 2013 and trade in 2014 was more or less static at a total value of $312.44 billion, after a decline of 5.1 % in 2013.[11] Some sectors such as Japan's sales of automobiles or consumer products have again recovered. The Chinese market is certainly too important for many Japanese companies to leave. But the two crises have shown Japanese business how easily another political crisis can negatively impact them.

More important for an appreciation of the potential of economic interdependence mediating conflict and tensions are the diametrically opposed perceptions in both countries of their interdependence which became particularly obvious during the 2012 confrontation. While many Chinese commentators and experts were seen to overrate Japan's vulnerability, their Japanese counterparts often showed a tendency to look at economic interdependence too much in purely economic terms, neglecting the impact of Chinese emotions and government propaganda, as well as the wider public's insufficient knowledge of the overall impact of bad economic relations with Japan on China's own economy.[12] The Japanese perception that China in the end needs Japan more than the other way round lingers on and is arguably correct in view of China's huge economic problems and needs, its dependence on Japanese high technology components for its manufacturing industry and environmental protection, and the dependence of the Chinese government's legitimacy on meeting the people's economic expectations. There is therefore a tendency to believe that despite recurring political crises in the relationship, China would, in the end, compromise, as it had done several times in the past.[13] Yet the problem with the perception of "China needing Japan" is, as the two crises in 2010 and 2012 have shown, that it can be politically manipulated, particularly in an authoritarian system. This gap between Japanese and Chinese observers and experts on the issue of dependence can seriously influence the willingness of both sides to compromise.[14] The escalation of the territorial conflict since 2012 from a stand-off between police forces (i.e. coast guards) to military forces and continued Chinese intrusions into the territorial waters around the islands has shown that the mediating role of continued economic interdependence cannot diminish the urgency of crisis management measures.

In contrast, in the case of the EEZ border confrontation between South Korea and China, economic interdependence still plays a stronger role since South Korea—a much smaller country—is economically so much more dependent on China than Japan. Seoul's careful handling of the EEZ dispute (confrontation with Chinese fishermen in the disputed EEZ, protracted negotiations over the EEZ demarcation, notably involving Ieodo/Suyan rock) but also other bilateral issues (North Korea, Chinese treatment of North Korean refugees and Chinese Koreans in Yanbian, ownership of the history of Goguryeo) is to a large extent due to South Korea's dependence on the Chinese market for trade and outsourcing.[15] China is South Korea's largest trading partner and their bilateral trade grew to $228.9bn in 2013.[16] South Korean investment in China is rapidly increasing, 90 % of which is in the manufacturing sector.[17] There are, of course, other non-economic reasons such as

South Korea's expectations regarding China playing a constructive role in curbing North Korean militancy (e.g. Six Party Talks).

IS THERE A TERRITORIAL PROBLEM BETWEEN JAPAN AND CHINA OR NOT?

Since 2012 China's objective seems to be to escalate tensions in order to make Japan recognise that there is a territorial conflict which for political/ legal reasons Japan denies. As the author has explained previously, it is only since the beginning of the 1990s that the Japanese government is explicitly denying that there is a territorial problem.[18] Moreover, the Japanese government has also been denying since then that there was an understanding in 1972 (establishment of diplomatic relations) and in 1978 (conclusion of the bilateral Peace and Friendship Treaty) to shelve (referred to in Japanese as "tana age" or "gezhi" in Chinese) the territorial issue. From the existing Japanese and Chinese literature it is obvious that there was such an understanding between the political leaders at the time although it was never made public in an official document and it is therefore easy to deny. In the above quoted article this author investigated the indications for the existence of such an understanding as well as the factors which eroded it over time. It was an understanding to agree to disagree, based on the mutual recognition that the positions of both countries on the sovereignty over the Senkaku/Diaoyu islands were diametrically opposite and that in the interest of the wider picture of the bilateral relationship, it was better not to touch it. It was an advantageous situation for Japan since it basically left the status quo, i.e. Japan's effective control over the islands, untouched although not unchallenged. Changes in the domestic politics of both countries (notably the rise of non-governmental actors), economic interests (such as hydrocarbon resources in the East China Sea), the legal implications of the ratification of UNCLOS by both countries in 1996 and military developments undermined the never clearly defined status quo around the islands dispute and finally led to the confrontations in 2010 and 2012 which has seriously aggravated the bilateral relationship and made constructively addressing the dispute so much more urgent but also so much more difficult. In addition—just at a time when Japan has a government under Prime Minister Abe with rather controversial ideas about the "history issue"—the Chinese government is weaving the islands conflict into its narrative of Japan's aggression against China. It is not only stating that Japan's aggression started with its incorporation of the islands in 1895, but is now also asserting that the 2012 government purchase of three of the islands is an "attempt to reverse the outcome of the Second World War."

A problem cannot be resolved or positively addressed in any way if one side even denies the existence of it. Moreover it makes it easy for China to undermine the credibility of Japan's stance because the stand-off between the policing and military forces of both sides can only leave the external observers with the obvious impression that there is a problem which moreover indirectly threatens the interests of surrounding countries. Moreover, the Japanese stance looks less persuasive since it is the reverse mirror image of Japan's position on the territorial dispute with South Korea over the Takeshima/Dokto Island in the Sea of Japan. Unfortunately refusing to recognise the existence of a territorial problem is often the default position of a government in control of a disputed territory. Although Japan can certainly receive some sympathies from its friends by pointing at China's coercive diplomacy, China—particularly in view of its growing economic and political importance against Japan's relative decline—can present its demand for the recognition of a territorial problem as a reasonable stance in contrast to Japan's stance.

In theory stating the recognition of the existence of a "territorial/border problem" or of "different opinions" on a given territory/border should not be difficult because it can always be supplemented by a qualifying sentence that such a statement in no way prejudices the legal position of the government. So far this has only been possible in relation to the yet not agreed EEZ border in the ECS. Such a qualifying statement is, for example, included in the Japan-China exchange of verbal notes for prior notification of research vessels from both countries in the East China Sea on 13 February 2001 (Article 6) where both sides wanted to reduce tensions arising from Chinese research vessels in an EEZ area claimed by both China and Japan without wanting to define the exact area. A similar qualification is part of the 1997 Japan-China Fisheries Agreement.[19]

Regarding arrangements pending the agreed demarcation of EEZ border, UNCLOS in Article 83 (3) provides that the provisional arrangements of a practical nature pending delimitation "shall be without prejudice to the final delimitation." Moreover, Japan and China have left open in their respective national legislation regarding their EEZ that the borders should be determined by mutual agreement as is required in Article 74 (3) of UNCLOS.[20]

DIPLOMATIC ACROBATICS FOR RECOGNIZING THE EXISTENCE OF A TERRITORIAL ISSUE

While finding a legal escape hole for the recognition of a Japan-China territorial issue is relatively straightforward, both sides will also have to find a face-saving wording. Moreover, the recognition of a territorial problem would be relatively easy to accept by Japanese public opinion (and even more so by Japan's friends and allies) because they would not see the need for any kind of diplomatic or legal sophistry for what is obviously a territorial conflict, whatever the legitimacy of the Chinese claim might be. According to a survey conducted by Genron together with Zhongguo Ribaoshe in 2014, 50.4 % (2013: 53.2%) of the Japanese gave the Senkaku issue as the reason for their unfavourable impression of China. Asked about what came to their mind when thinking of China, 28.6 % (2013: 34.1 %) of the Japanese mentioned in the third place the Senkaku issue.[21]

Diplomacy is about finding wordings which sometimes can reconcile apparently irreconcilable interests. There have been several attempts by Japanese politicians to find a wording which circumvent the risk of being perceived as admitting the existence of a territorial problem. The deputy prime minister of the previous Noda government, Okada Katsuya, was reported to have mentioned in a speech in October 2012 that there was no territorial dispute but as a matter of fact "a debate existed."[22] However, this compromise solution was never confirmed by the Noda government and did not become policy. Among influential opinion makers there is hardly any support for admitting the existence of a territorial conflict or of a shelving agreement. At the same time he emphasised, however, that there was no territorial dispute. Japan Business Federation Chairman Yonekura Hiromasa mentioned in September 2012 in an NHK interview that the government should be more flexible since otherwise its stance could be taken to mean that Japan has no intention of solving the dispute.[23] Miyamoto Yuji, the former Japanese ambassador to China, is quoted as saying that 'The government does not need to alter its basic position, but in reality, a conflict does exist over the Senkaku isles'.[24] This is also the stance which the previous Japanese ambassador Niwa Uichiro in Beijing takes in an article after his return to Japan.[25]

The separate statements by both governments on 7 November 2014 just before the APEC summit meeting in Beijing signalled a certain movement on the issue of admitting the existence of a territorial issue. There were incentives on both sides to be more flexible: As the host of the summit meeting in Beijing, Xi Jingping could not easily refuse a meeting of any kind with Japan's prime minister Abe as one of the representatives of a major APEC member state without paying a diplomatic price towards all other member states, notably those involved in the stand-off about the South China Sea dispute. At the same time a meeting provided the former with a lever to extract from Abe a compromise on his "no-territorial-conflict" stance as well as on the history issue. Prime Minister Abe on his part was keen to have a meeting with Xi in order to restart bilateral discussions on a whole range of common interests.

However, the outcome of rather intensive preparatory diplomatic negotiations was not even a joint statement but rather two separate statements which differed in subtle ways. Moreover, each side published the English version of its statement on their own without consultation while making their respective emphasis even clearer in the English version than in the original language versions.[26] The Chinese version is titled "China and Japan Reach Four-Point Principled Agreement (gongshi) on Handling and Improving Bilateral Relations" whereas the Japanese text is titled "Regarding Discussions toward Improving Japan-China Relations" which indicated that the Japanese side did not consider it as an agreement with the ensuing binding connotation. Whereas the Chinese version regarding the differences regarding the disputed islands reads that both sides "acknowledged (renshi) that different positions exist between them regarding the tensions which have emerged in recent years over the Diaoyu Islands and some waters in the East China Sea," the Japanese is weaker and says only that "both sides recognized (ninshiki suru) that they had different views as to the emergence of tense situations in recent years in the waters of the East China Sea, including those around the Senkaku Islands." Moreover the statements try to avoid any particular focus on the islands themselves by referring to the East China Sea in general including the Senkaku/Diaoyu Islands (Senkaku shotto nado Higashi Shinakaiiki ni oite/ weirao Diaoyudao deng Donghai haijin).[27] That the Senkaku Islands dispute is only one among other issues in the East China Sea was several days later driven home by Foreign Minister Kishida Fumio when he mentioned other issues like the ADIZ and the exploitation of seabed resources.[28]

Can this 7 November statement therefore be interpreted as a Japanese recognition that there is a "territorial issue" between the two countries? Whereas Chinese official interpretations went into this direction, the Japanese government quickly explained that this statement did not imply any change of Japan's stance and that it had moreover no binding force but should only be "respected."[29] This Japanese interpretation was strongly criticised by a spokesman of the Chinese embassy in Tokyo.[30] In theory the 7th November statement could be a face-saving first step to manage and later even solve the islands dispute if both government are seeing an improvement of the relationship in their overriding interest. Although recognizing the existence of a territorial problem, even in the most convoluted way, is not necessarily leading to a new shelving of it, the 7 November 2014 statements led to both sides gradually resuming political, diplomatic and security dialogues. Most relevant for the discussion here is that both versions of the statements speak of the intention to establish crisis management mechanisms to avoid incidents and the resumption of high-level talks. Talks about crisis managements mechanisms have since then occurred.

FROM CONFLICT MANAGEMENT TO CONFLICT PREVENTION

The establishment of crisis management mechanisms between two countries Japan and China (and this is also true for China and South Korea as well as China and the US) is fraught with many difficulties given the very different security apparatuses on both sides (e.g. who is to pick up the phone at the other side and who can then make a decision?) and the number of actors (air and maritime forces, coast guards, etc). An even more fundamental problem is the Chinese understanding of a crisis management mechanism as a sign of weakness and capitulation, but also as a lever to extract prior concessions.[31] As the history of the establishment of a hotline between the two sides since 1998 has shown, China requested a better atmosphere conducive to talks about the establishment of the hotline, and broke off discussions just when the existence of a hotline was most required as in 2010 and 2012.[32] In 2015 it is particularly the handling of the 70th anniversary of the end of war by Japan and China which hangs as a Damocles sword over the resumption of negotiations.

Even with South Korea the establishment of a hotline has been delayed although it is more advanced than between Japan and China. In 2008, South Korea's Second Fleet Headquarters established a hotline with China's North Sea Fleet Headquarters in Qingdao, and the South Korean Air Force's master control and reporting centre with the air defence centre in China's Jinan Military Region. However, for various technical and other reasons, its value as a military communication system is rather low.[33] In 2014 an MOU was signed by both sides to establish a hotline between the defence ministries by the end of 2014 and at a meeting in February 2015 this was reported to the first half of 2015.[34]

As a first step, such a crisis management mechanism should allow appropriate communication between all relevant actors in case of an incident, which may range from an alleged infraction by a fishing boat to an aerial encounter of military aircraft. However, crisis management is in the end not enough and—as in the case with the 2008 South Korea-China hotline—would only end up in the mere exchange of opposing statements by each side if such a management mechanism is not ultimately followed up by crisis prevention measures. For prevention, rules of engagement have to be agreed upon which are binding despite the difficulty arising from differences on territorial issues and EEZ borders. In exchange for Japan making a compromise on the recognition of the existence of a territorial problem along the lines proposed above, China would have to reciprocate with desisting from coercive diplomacy. To prevent incidents, measures have to be taken which reduce the risk of a military clash, but in a way which prevents the perception that one side is giving in to coercion. This stage would see a gradual phasing out of intrusions by Chinese official vessels and aircraft into the Territorial

Waters, Contiguous Zone and airspace of the disputed islands, which is reciprocated by Japan's reducing in the same way its coastguard patrols in the two zones, as well as its scrambling activities in the islands' airspace.[35] While it is too early to evaluate the chances of this to happen in the aftermath of the 7th November 2014 statements, the initial signs were not good: Since then (as of March 2015), there have been ten intrusions of Chinese Coast Guard ships into the Territorial Waters of the islands while during the rest of the time, these ships have been cruising in the Contiguous Zone (12-24 nm from the islands) which has been broadly the pattern since 2010.[36] Incidentally, China had proposed to Japan in June 2013 to agree to a 12-nautical-mile no-entry zone around the islands.[37] Japan rejected this proposal because it was linked to China demanding from Japan to acknowledge the existence of a territorial problem.

Ultimately rules of engagement have to be agreed upon between all parties in the East China Sea which do not only concern the waters and airspace around the disputed islands but the whole ECS. One partial step was taken in April 2014 with the signing of the Code for Unplanned Encounters at Sea (CUES) by the naval chiefs of 25 states—including China, Japan and the US—at the Western Pacific Naval Symposium (WPNS) in Qingdao. However, it will be only of limited use for the ECS since it is not legally binding, does not apply to territorial waters, and China understands it to include only the High Seas.[38] However, the Code contains important elements which could be incorporated into bilateral agreements among the three ECS countries.

One important rule to prevent incidents would be to increase the distance at which vessels of maritime forces observe each other as part of an ever extending code of conduct and rules of engagement. Such steps should ultimately be officialised by a gradually expanding series of Confidence and Security Building Measures (CSBM). This could also include a demilitarisation agreement of the disputed islands as an incentive for the Chinese side. It would be vital that the steps at this stage be incremental, that no step is exploited in a one-sided way, and that they are considered irreversible. At the same time both sides have to prevent people from approaching the islands, since this would be seen as a provocation by the other side. This latter task is technically not easy because of the controversial character of any compromise for certain non-state actors in Japan, China, Hong Kong and Taiwan who consider their own government's stance on the islands as being too soft. The (failed) landing of a Chinese hot balloonist near one of the islands in January 2014 demonstrated at the same time the technical difficulty of enforcing a no-entry policy even for an authoritarian regime like that of China as well as the possibility of a successful cooperation of the coastguards of Taiwan, Japan and China which rescued the balloonist.[39]

All these carefully scripted steps which would have to take into account face and legal sensitivities will require leadership and good will. It is therefore absolutely necessary that Japan refrains from measures which would be perceived as provocative by China and sometimes do not even obtain the understanding of Japan's allies (e.g. the visit of the Yasukuni Shrine by political leaders or the revision of the Murayama Statement on the war prostitutes). China would have to reciprocate by considerably toning down its patriotic campaign which now constantly evokes through films, propaganda campaigns, memorial events etc. Japan's aggression against China before 1945 and totally ignores Japan's peaceful policies since then. China will also have to be more forthcoming on agreeing to CSBMs, and not merely consider them as political levers to obtain prior concessions, which totally perverts the meaning and intention of CSBMs.

THE SOVEREIGNTY ISSUE

The most sensitive problem is the sovereignty issue which goes to the core of any country's security interests. It is not imaginable that either side will simply renounce its claim to the islands. However, both sides have "stains" on their sovereignty claim as the author has previously explained: The circumstances of Japan's acquisition may be strong in terms of international law at the time but certain historical circumstances cast a political and moral shadow over it, while China's total silence between 1895 and 1970 about its claim and the timing of making the claim in the wake of the discovery of oil and gas around the disputed islands considerably weaken its legal position.[40] These caveats should lead both sides to some humility and make them more amenable to find a compromise, apart from all the dangers of the current tensions and stand-off. Sidestepping or shelving the territorial issue is only useful if the lessons from the failed attempts in 1972 and 1978 can be learned. However, shelving does not address the fundamental problem inherent in its implicit assumption that the quality of the bilateral relationship will always be as good as when the sidestepping agreement was achieved, and that this quality can be maintained in perpetuity, or at least until the sovereignty issue can be solved. In fact, an even better quality of the relationship has to be created in order to achieve a compromise over the sovereignty issue which had not been possible when the problem was merely shelved.

An important step towards resolving the territorial issue is reducing the value of the islands for both countries by resolutely preventing anyone from approaching the territories (including total demilitarization) as proposed above for crisis prevention. This would have to include the territorial waters and the exploitation there of any kind of resources including fishing. The most difficult part here as mentioned before is to prevent any act by non-governmental actors. One major advantage of the Senkaku/Diaoyu Islands dispute is that there are no inhabitants on these islands, in contrast to the territorial disputes over Gibraltar or the Falklands/Malvinas which are often mentioned in comparison. Closely linked in importance is the prevention of any governmental act which could be interpreted as being part of the "sovereignty game." Scientific interests in the islands could be served by bilateral surveys without any political connotations. There have been proposals to declare the islands an International Nature and Wildlife Preserve.[41] Such a preserve would have to be administered either bilaterally or by a relevant international organisation and as such could serve as a confidence-building measure.

The above steps would then allow the two sides to deal with the considerable economic interests in fishing and the exploitation of hydrocarbon resources and other seabed resources around the islands, i.e. in the EEZ and/or the Extended Continental Shelf. Once the islands' land area and the territorial waters have been put aside, it would be easier to come to an overall agreement on the delimitation of the EEZ border (with the exception of the northern part which would require a trilateral agreement between China, Japan and Korea). If both sides agreed that the islands do not generate their own EEZ or continental shelf claims, the facilitation of delimitating the EEZ border between Japan and China would also be a helpful step for addressing the sovereignty issue.[42] This renunciation of an EEZ around the islands might be difficult to accept for Japan which claims an EEZ for Okinotorishima, refuted by China since it considers the reef not to be an island according to the criteria of Art. 121 of UNCLOS. Moreover, some of the Senkaku/Diaoyu Islands were inhabited for some time before 1941 which fulfils one criteria for being acknowledged as islands and thus qualifying for an EEZ.

A compromise on the sovereignty issue could only be the outcome—if at all—of a successful process of the above or comparable steps. In order to avoid a "winner take all" situation, the compromise would have to involve some kind of sharing arrangement. History and contemporary international relations offer quite a number of approaches, such as shared sovereignty referred to as condominium in international law, alternating sovereignty, international zones, internationalisation (Antarctica), or division.[43] The Chinese international lawyer Guo Rongxin discusses five different options for a territorial dispute settlement: 1) fair division scheme 2) joint management scheme 3) international peace park 4) neutral zone 5) buffer zone and 6) demilitarized zone.[44] Hashimoto Akikazu, Michael O'Hanlon and Wu Xinbo proposed in a recent article to temporarily freeze the sovereignty issue over the Senkaku/Diaoyu Islands and to share administrative duties and rights over the islands.[45]

Europe provides a very special example of a condominium, involving even today alternating sovereignty every six months between France and

Spain over a small island (3,000 square meters) in the river in the Basque region separating France and Spain, known as Pheasant Island. Like the Senkaku/Diaoyu Islands, the island has no economic value anymore, and the island is off limits. It was the location of the signing of the Treaty of the Pyrenees in 1659 which ended a long war and has since then become a symbol of Franco-Spanish reconciliation.[46] Most other examples of joint sovereignty concern territories with a population, which makes cooperation much more difficult. Other historical precedents of sharing sovereignty are the establishment of neutral zones. Accordingly, the islands themselves and possibly a sea area around the islands could be declared a neutral zone like the one between Saudi Arabia and Kuwait (1922-1965). On July 7, 1965, these two governments signed an agreement (which took effect on July 25, 1966) to partition the Neutral Zone adjoining their respective territories. A demarcation agreement dividing the Neutral Zone was signed on December 17, 1967. Particularly relevant here is that Saudi Arabia as well as Kuwait exploited the oil resources under a joint operating agreement.[47]

Division is also a possibility as it was proposed in 2007 by then Foreign Minister Aso Taro in the context of solving the so-called disputed Southern Kurile Islands (called Northern Territories by Japan). Where to draw the dividing line between the Senkaku/Diaoyu Islands could be informed by the chronology of Japan's acquisition of these islands. Accordingly Japan would cede Kubajima and Uotsurijima, which were the only islands incorporated into Japan in January 1895, and Japan keeps those like Taishojima and some other little islands which were only incorporated in 1921.[48]

CONCLUSIONS

The action-reaction pattern in the Senkaku/Diaoyu Islands dispute is still continuing despite a potentially promising development with the two statements of 7th November 2014. In addition, the establishment of an ADIZ by China in December 2013 has heightened further tensions in the whole ECS not only with Japan, but also with South Korea and the US, worsening the atmosphere even for the establishment of an agreed EEZ border between all three East Asian countries.

Washington's East Asia policy is torn between the intention of maintaining its supremacy in the region which relies substantially on its security treaty links with both Japan and South Korea, and protecting considerable political and economic interests in a good relationship with China. The role of the US in the territorial dispute is therefore confined to provide a military deterrent against any Chinese military actions and to exhort all players to have dialogue and agree on measures to enhance confidence. There are indications that the US Administration is not only dissatisfied with China's coercive diplomacy in the territorial conflict, but also with Japan's rigid position. Although the US security guarantee which explicitly includes the disputed islands was officially strengthened when President Obama as the first US president repeated it on his Japan visit in April 2014, there is some dissatisfaction in Japan in view of Washington's refusal to pronounce itself on the sovereignty of the islands.[49] This American position naturally raises doubts about the reliability of the US security guarantee because it would be unusual to fight for a territory whose sovereignty is considered undetermined. This situation of US dissatisfaction with Japan's approach to China as well as Japanese doubts about the US security guarantee—in addition to concerns about the tensions in the ECS—should encourage Tokyo to be more proactive in searching for means of crisis management, conflict prevention and possibly resolution of the sovereignty issue as discussed above. The diverging power trajectories of Japan and China should be a further encouragement for Japan's leaders to achieve a political compromise sooner rather than later.

There are also strong incentives for China to establish agreed EEZ borders and to address the territorial conflict in the ECS. It is not in China's interest to be seen as increasing tensions with its two East Asian neighbours and challenging the international norm of the inviolability of national sovereignty. The more it uses coercive means, the more it loses international credibility and raises fears about its other territorial demands, notably in the South China Sea. Provoking regional anti-China coalition building is not helpful for China's development. China needs a peaceful accommodation with the US, and the ECS is a vital part of this endeavour.

Both Japan and China need a committed leadership which understands the "wider picture" as both sides are fond to reiterate!

NOTES

1. "South Korea vows 'firm action' over China's claim on submerged rock," Mainichi, March 12, 2012, http://mdn.mainichi.jp/mdnnews/international/news/20120312p2g00m0in160000c.html (no longer accessible, copy with author).

2. "Senkaku shoto shuhen kaiiki ni okeru Chugoku kosento no doko to waga kuni no taisho (The movements of Chinese government vessels in the area of the Senkaku Islands and the countermeasures of Japan)," Japan Coast Guard, accessed March 18, 2015, http://www.kaiho.mlit.go.jp/senkaku/.

3. John Garnaut, Sydney Morning Herald, July 3, 2014, accessed March 21, 2015, www.smh.com.au/world/brace-for-more-tensions-in-asia-chinese-analyst-20140703-zsudd.html.

4. Minxin Pei, "China and Japan Beware: World War I's Lesson for the East China Sea," National Interest, July 1, 2014, accessed March 18, 2015, http://nationalinterest.org/feature/china-japan-beware-world-war-lesson-the-east-china-sea-10780?page=1.

5. Koichiro Genba, "Japan-China Relations at a Crossroads," New York Times, Nov. 21, 2011, accessed March 18, 2015, www.nytimes.com/2012/11/21/opinion/koichiro-genba-japan-china-relations-at-a-crossroads.html?ref=japan.

6. Andrew Chubb, "Exploring China's 'Maritime Consciousness'," Public Opinion on the South and East China Sea Disputes (Perth: USAsian Centre, 2014), p. 41.

7. Interview with a high official of the Japanese Ministry of Foreign Affairs, May 28, 2008.

8. "Settlement of Disputes Mechanism," United Nations, accessed March 18, 2015, www.un.org/Depts/los/settlement_of_disputes/choice_procedure.htm.

9. Chengyi Lin, "Lingering territorial dispute and Taiwan-US-China relations," Ajia Ken-kyu 58, no. 4 (October 2012), pp. 25-36.

10. Reinhard Drifte, "The Senkaku/Diaoyu Islands Territorial Dispute between Japan and China. Between the Materialization of the 'China Threat' and 'Reversing the Outcome of World War II'?" UNISCI Discussion Papers 32 (Complutense University of Madrid, May 2013), pp. 45-46, accessed March 21, 2015, http://pendientedemigracion.ucm.es/info/unisci/revistas/UNISCIDP32-1DRIFTE.pdf.

11. "Japan's Investment in China," Yomiuri Shimbun Japan News, http://e-japan-news.com/news/article/0001859934 (no longer accessible, copy with author). "China-Japan Trade Flat in 2014," MarketPulse, January 13, 2015, accessed March 18, 2015, http://www.marketpulse.com/20150113/china-japan-trade-flat-2014/.

12. For examples of overrating see Wu, Di, Caijing, Sept. 9, 2012, quoted in: Martina Bassan, "China's Strategy towards Japan in the Diaoyu Island Dispute,"China Analysis, February 27, 2013, accessed March 18, 2015, http://www.ecfr.eu/page/-/China_Analysis_Shockwaves_from_the_China_Japan_Island_Dispute_February2013.pdf, pp. 9-10.

13. Reinhard Drifte, "The Future of the Japanese-Chinese Relationship: The Case for a Grand Political Bargain'," Asia-Pacific Review 16, no. 2 (2009), p. 56.

14. "Factory shift to non-Chinese sites seen accelerating. Companies reopen as anger eases in China," Japan Times, Sept. 21, 2012, accessed March 21, 2015, http://www.japantimes.co.jp/text/nb20120921a1.html.

15. For the territorial issues see "As Cold War glaciers melt, Chinese-Korean tensions may grow more pronounced." Andrew S. Erickson and Michael Monti, February 20, 2015, accessed March 21, 2015, http://nationalinterest.org/feature/trouble-ahead-chinese-korean-disputes-may-intensify-12284?page=1 to 7.

16. "China and South Korea are set to sign a Free Trade Agreement that aims to remove most Barriers to Trade between the two Countries," BBC News, November 10, 2014, accessed March 18, 2015, http://www.bbc.co.uk/news/business-29983756.

17. Kazunori Takada and Sohee Kim, "South Korean Firms, unfazed by slowing Economy, step up China Investment," Reuters, October 21, 2014, accessed March 18, 2015, www.reuters.com/article/2014/10/22/china-southkorea-fdi-idUSL3N0SF2LU20141022.

18. Reinhard Drifte, "The Japan-China Confrontation Over the Senkaku/Diaoyu Islands—Between 'shelving' and 'dispute escalation'," The Asia-Pacific Journal 12, issue 30, no. 3 (July 28, 2014), accessed March 21, 2015, http://japanfocus.org/-Reinhard-Drifte/4154.

19. Text of Notes received from the Japanese Ministry of Foreign Affairs. Text of Fishery Agreement: "Gyogyo ni kan suru Nihonkoku to Chuka Jinmin Kyowakoku to no aida no kyotei (Agreement on fishing between Japan and the People`s Republic of China)" (entered into force June 1, 2000), accessed March 18, 2015, www.mofa.go.jp/mofaj/gaiko/treaty/pdfs/A-H12-343.pdf, p. 352 Art. 12.

20. United Nations, "China: Exclusive Economic Zone and Continental Shelf Act 26 June 1998," Article 2, un.org/Depts/los/LEGISLATIONANDTREATIES/PDFFILES/chn-1998-eez-act.pdf. United Nations, "Law on the Exclusive Economic Zone and the Continental Shelf of Japan," Article 2(1), both accessed March 18, 2015, www.un.org/Depts/los/LEGISLATION-ANDTREATIES/PDFFILES/JPN_1996_Law74.pdf.

21. "Genron Survey," September 2014, accessed March 21, 2015, www.genron-npo.net/en/pp/docs/10th_Japan-China_poll.pdf.

22. Teddy Ng, "Japan's deputy PM admits Diaoyu dispute, opening path to China talks, South China Morning Post , Oct. 23, 2012, accessed March 18, 2015, http://www.scmp.com/news/asia/article/1067564/japans-deputy-pm-admits-diaoyus-dispute-opening-path-china-talks.

23. "Yonekura urges flexibility by Japan over Senkakus," NHK, Sept. 28, 2012, http://www3.nhk.or.jp/daily/english/20120928_36.html, (no longer accessible, copy with author).

24. "Ex-ambassador to China calls for Senkakus talks," Japan Times , Sept. 27, 2012.

25. Uichiro Niwa, "Nitchu gaiko no shinjitsu (The truth of Japan-China diplomacy)," Bungei Shunju (February 2013): pp. 120-31.

26. Nozomu Hayashi, "Even on agreement document, Japan, China quarrelled over English phrasing," Asahi Shimbun, Nov. 22, 2014, accessed March 20, 2015, http://ajw.asahi.com/article/behind_news/politics/AJ201411220041.

27. Japanese statement: "Regarding Discussions toward Improving Japan-China Relations," Ministry of Foreign Affairs of Japan, Nov. 7, 2014, http://www.mofa.go.jp/a_o/c_m1/cn/page4e_000150.html. "Nicchu kankei no kaizen ni muketa no hanashiai (Discussions for the improvement of Japan-China relations)," Ministry of Foreign Affairs of Japan, Nov. 7, 2014, http://www.mofa.go.jp/mofaj/a_o/c_m1/cn/page4_000789.html. Chinese statement: "Yang Jiechi meets National Security Advisor Shotaro Yachi. China and Japan Reach Four-Point Principled Agreement on Handling and Improving Bilateral Relations," November 7, 2014, Ministry of Foreign Affairs of the People's Republic of China. "Yang Jiechi huijian Riben guojia anquan baozhang juzhang Shotaro Yachi (Meeting of Yang Jiechi with the head of Japan's National Security Council Shotaro Yachi)," Ministry of Foreign Affairs of the People's Republic of China, Nov. 7, 2014, http://www.fmprc.gov.cn/mfa_eng/zxxx_662805/t1208360.shtml. Press Conference by Minister of Foreign Affairs Fumio Kishida, Ministry of Foreign Affairs of Japan, Nov. 11, 2014, www.mofa.go.jp/press/kaiken/kaiken4e_000123.html. All accessed March 20, 2015.

28. Press Conference by Minister of Foreign Affairs Fumio Kishida, Nov. 11, 2014, accessed March 21, 2015, www.mofa.go.jp/press/kaiken/kaiken4e_000123.html.

29. Nozomu Hayashi, et. al, "Japan, China both claim advantage in pre-summit document," Asahi Shimbun, Nov. 8, 2014, http://ajw.asahi.com/article/behind_news/politics/AJ201411080037. Press Conference by Minister of Foreign Affairs Fumio Kishida, Ministry of Foreign Affairs of Japan, Nov. 13, 2014, http://english.kyodonews.jp/news/2014/11/322208.html (both accessed March 20, 2015).

30. People Daily, accessed March 21, 2015, http://english.peopledaily.com.cn/n/2014/1113/c90883-8808160.html.

31. M. Duchâtel and F. Huijskens, "The European Union's principled neutrality on the East China Sea," SIPRI Policy Brief (February 2015): 6, accessed March 21, 2015, http://books.sipri.org/product_info?c_product_id=493.

32. Tuosheng Zhang, "Building trust between China and Japan: lessons learned from bilateral interactions in the East China Sea," SIPRI Policy Brief, February 2015, fn 5, accessed March 21, 2015, http://books.sipri.org/product_info?c_product_id=492.

33. "S Korea, China expected to set up military hotline this year: source," Yonhap, July 20, 2014, accessed March 21, 2015, http://english.yonhapnews.co.kr/full/2014/07/18/44/1200000000AEN20140718008800315F.html.

34. Yoon Sukjoon, "The Proposed Defense Ministry Hotline Between China and South Korea," The Diplomat, Feb. 17, 2015, accessed March 21, 2015, http://thediplomat.com/2015/02/the-proposed-defense-ministry-hotline-between-china-and-south-korea/.

35. For more detailed proposals see Zhang, Tuosheng, op. cit., p. 5.

36. For more precise details of incursions see the Japanese site www.kaiho.mlit.go.jp/senkaku/ and the Chinese site www.diaoyudao.org.cn/node_7217868.htm (only since Jan. 27, 2014).

37. "China set summit precondition for Japan: Declare no-entry zone around Senkakus," Japan Times, June 22, 2013, accessed March 21, 2015, www.japantimes.co.jp/news/2013/06/22/national/china-set-summit-precondition-for-japan-declare-no-entry-zone-around-senkakus/#.UcWVUNjnT5k.

38. O. Bräuner, J. Chan, and F. Huijskens, "Confrontation and cooperation in the East China Sea: Chinese perspectives," SIPRI Policy Brief, (February 2015): 5, accessed March 21, 2015, http://books.sipri.org/product_info?c_product_id=492.

39. "Japan rescues ditched Chinese balloonist," Global Times, Jan. 3, 2014, accessed March 21, 2015, www.globaltimes.cn/content/835527.shtml.

40. Reinhard Drifte, "The Senkaku/Diaoyu Islands Territorial Dispute between Japan and China. Between the Materialization of the 'China Threat' and 'Reversing the Outcome of World War II'?" UNISCI Discussion Papers no. 32 (Complutense University of Madrid, May

2013): 9-62, accessed March 21, 2015, http://pendientedemigracion.ucm.es/info/unisci/revistas/UNISCIDP32-1DRIFTE.pdf.

41. James J. Przystup and Phillip C. Saunders, "Time for China and Japan to cool it," March 1, 2013, accessed March 21, 2015, http://www.asiasentinel.com/politics/time-for-china-and-japan-to-cool-it/.

42. Not giving the islands an EEZ to facilitate the delimitation of an EEZ border is apparently the general academic opinion in China: Gong Yingchun, "The development and current status of maritime disputes in the East China Sea," National Bureau of Asian Research, NBR Special Report 35 (December 2011), p. 113.

43. Joel H. Samuels, "Condominium Arrangements in International Practice: Reviving an Abandoned Concept of Boundary Dispute Resolution," 29 Michigan Journal of International Law 727 (2008). For a list of condominiums see http://en.wikipedia.org/wiki/Condominium_%28international_law%29.

44. Guo Rongxing, "Territorial disputes and conflict management. The art of avoiding war," Chapter 3 (London: Routledge 2012), pp. 85-171.

45. Akikazu Hashimoto, Michael O'Hanlon and Wu Xinbo, "A framework for resolving Japan-China dispute over islands," Los Angeles Times, Dec. 2, 2013, accessed March 21, 2015, www.brookings.edu/research/opinions/2014/12/02-japan-china-island-dispute-ohanlon?hs_u.

46. Jean-Paul Pancracio, "Un condominium sur la Bidassoa," June 5, 2012, http://blogs.univ-poitiers.fr/jp-pancracio/tag/ile-des-faisans/. This example was also raised by the Japanese political scientist Naka Norio: Naka Norio, Ryodo mondai kara, kokkyo gakutei mondai (Tokyo: Akashi Shoten 2013), p. 312. For other condominiums see Frank Jacobs, "The world's most exclusive condominium," International New York Times, Jan. 23, 2012, http://opinionator.blogs.nytimes.com/2012/01/23/the-worlds-most-exclusive-condominium/?_php=true&_type=blogs&_r=0, all accessed March 20, 2015.

47. Mohd. Talaat El Ghoneimy, "The Legal Status of the Saudi-Kuwaiti Neutral Zone," The International and Comparative Law Quarterly 15, no. 3, July 1966.

48. Norio Naka, op. cit., pp. 252-54.

49. Yoshiki Mine, "President Obama's Comments on the Senkaku Islands," May 19, 2014, www.canon-igs.org/en/column/security/20140519_2576.html, accessed March 20, 2015.

Chapter Five

Juggling Triads

Australian Foreign Policy towards Japan and China

David Walton, Senior Lecturer,
Western Sydney University

In many respects the bilateral relationships Australia is enjoying with both Japan and China is at an all-time high. Prime Ministerial-led initiatives by Tony Abbot and reciprocal visits in 2014 to both countries are indicative of the intent to strengthen already robust bilateral relationships. Nonetheless the rise of China and its impact on regional dynamics is one of the greatest challenges faced by Australian diplomats in a generation and has been the source of immense debate in Australia. In the case of Japan, the security communities in both countries are 'on side' and committed to expanding the security ties. Notably, the signing of an Economic Partnership (EPA) in July 2014 and ratified by both parliaments in January 2015 is expected to lead to a substantial expansion in two-way trade. Australia's abundant natural gas reserves, moreover, are seen as a potential alternative energy supply for a post-Fukushima Japan wary of the use of nuclear power plants. Australia's relationship with China, however, is more problematic. The extraordinary rise of the Chinese economy has meant that China since 2008 has been Australia's largest trading partner. At the same time, China's strategic competition with the United States and the subsequent changing geo-political landscape, has led to more uncertainty in the Asia Pacific region. This chapter will critically examine both bilateral relations and Australia's response to the rise of China.

JAPAN: A STRATEGIC PARTNERSHIP

The current bilateral relationship between Australia and Japan is one of the longest and most stable partnerships in the post-war period. Based on complementarity in trade, post-war Australia-Japan ties were driven by commercial interests that were a catalyst for the expansion of ties in the political and security spheres. Much has been written about Japan's 'economic miracle' during the late 1960s to early 1980s that was, to some extent, underwritten by raw materials supplied from Australia. The resources boom and massive increase in investment in the minerals sector, in turn, was driven by Japan's high economic rates of growth. [1] These trade and commercial complementarities have been enhanced by the strong support for security alliance with the United States (US) and other important shared values such as retaining a strong US presence in the region, support for democracy, rule of law, human rights and free trade. In turn, these shared interests have led to substantial co-operation in regional diplomacy including joint initiatives to support the construction of regional architecture (APEC and East Asia Summit) and aid and development assistance programs in Southeast Asia. Australia and Japan have also jointly chaired nuclear disarmament efforts in the United Nations.

The most remarkable component of surging bilateral ties has been the rapid growth in security links since 2003. The legacy of the Pacific War (poor treatment of Australian POWs and direct threat of a Japanese invasion) in effect meant that Japanese officials were treated with hostility and distrust when diplomatic relations resumed in 1952. Nonetheless, post-war relations improved at a surprisingly fast pace. The aforementioned trade complementarities and each countries role as a 'spoke' in the US-led cold war structure were critical factors in the improvement in relations. Irregular and ad hoc political and security dialogue on regional issues began in earnest by the 1960s. Developments in Southeast Asia and Indonesia, in particular, were a critical issue and a source of dialogue and disagreement. [2] By the 1990s, the process of regular political consultation was institutionalised and upgraded to include military attaches and formal discussions on regional and global issues. As close allies of the US, the terrorist attacks on the US in September 11, 2001 were a catalyst for a substantial upgrade in co-operation, consultation and interoperability. Since 2003, Trilateral Security Dialogue (TSD) between the US, Japan and Australia has led to regular annual meetings (at the ministerial level since 2006) and joint military exercises in the South China Sea and elsewhere in the Asia Pacific region. Subsequent security upgrades have been centred on the Japan—Australia Declaration of Joint Security Co-operation (2007) and the 2009 Action Plan to implement the key points articulated in the declaration. In essence the declaration was not a security treaty but was designed to deal with common security interests such as border security, counter-terrorism, peace cooperation, exchange of information and personnel and joint exercises and coordinated activities. The regular Foreign Affairs and Defence meetings at the ministerial level known as 'Two Plus Two talks' were the most significant of these measures.[3] The inaugural ministerial talks were held in Tokyo in June 2007 and have since been held on an annual basis. Notably, this was the first of its kind for Japan (except with the US) and was based on the US-Japan dialogue model.

Combined with annual Trilateral Security Dialogue talks at the ministerial level between the United States, Japan and Australia, the security agreement has been viewed as a turning point in bilateral relations and has led to several security upgrades in subsequent years.[4] In 2010, for example, momentum included the Acquisition and Cross-Servicing Agreement (ACSA) signed in May (only second ACSA agreement signed by Japan). The agreement provided a framework for reciprocal provision of supplies and services between the JSDF and the ADF on exercises and training, UN Peace Keeping Operations and overseas disaster relief operations and came into effect in January 2013.[5] As noted by Cook and Wilkins, the momentum gained by these upgrades will continue to reverberate for the foreseeable future due to mutual defence concerns, the multiple opportunities for military cooperation and pressure from the United States, which is increasingly demanding more support from allies.[6]

The upgrades have led to a substantial growth in collaboration between Australian and Japanese defence personnel and have been well received in Tokyo. In December 2010, Japan's National Defence Policy Guidelines (NDPG), which represents the governments strategic defence strategy for the following ten years, reflected the new dimension in security ties with Australia stating "Japan will enhance security with countries such as South Korea, Australia, ASEAN and India."[7] Australia, in this context, is viewed as an important strategic partner aligned with the US and with shared strategic interest in the Asia Pacific region. According to Katahara, the Australia—Japan security relationship offers multiple benefits including facilitating Japan's move towards strategic normalcy and, in the context of a strengthened US alliance network, encouraging —China to act as a responsible stakeholder in the region and [in] the world at large.[8] The TSD talks have also facilitated closer coordination and along the lines expressed above. The June 2013 TSD joint statement, for example, highlighted the desire to strengthen trilateral cooperative efforts in information sharing, joint military training and exercise coordination.[9] Such coordination has led security commentators to argue that the Australia-Japan security relationship is in reality, a form of 'Bilateralism Plus'. The 'plus' factor refers to bilateral cooperation embedded in the wider formula of trilateral cooperation with the United States. This can be observed through annual TSD talks and the construction of security webs sponsored by the United States.[10]

At the time of writing, the Abbott – Abe conservative alliance has already led to intense discussion on further security upgrades in the area of interoperability and a framework for commitment in defence equipment and technology including enhanced training and joint exercises. The pace of development is reminiscent of changes during the years 2006/2007 under the Howard/Abe partnership. In April 2014, Abbott received much fanfare while in Tokyo and was the first foreign leader to address the newly formed National Security Council of Japan.[11] At the fifth 'Two plus Two' security dialogue in June that same year, agreement was reached to jointly develop defence equipment that could pave the way for Japan to send to Australia stealth submarine technology. During Abe's visit to Australia in July (6-9) 2014, the two leaders re-affirmed the strong growth in defence and security ties. Notably and much to the delight of Japanese policymakers, Abbott supported Japan's policy of a pro-active contribution to peace including the right to collective self-defense.[12] The momentum has not abated. During Foreign Minister Bishop's visit to Tokyo in May 2015, arrangements were made to allow the smooth passage of military personnel from both countries for military joint exercises.[13]

THE RISE OF CHINA AND COMPETING INTERESTS

Early post-war relations with China were viewed within the prism of cold war politics. Understandably, relations were severely strained and remained in a form of limbo until the Whitlam Government established diplomatic ties in December 1972. Notably the conservative Menzies Government in 1949 chose not to follow British foreign policy, which recognised the state of China but not the Communist Government in power, and instead endorsed the United States policy of recognising Taiwan as the legitimate China (and thereby making mainland China a pariah state). In opposition Gough Whitlam had consistently supported the recognition of The Peoples Republic of China (PRC) and demonstrated his commitment to normalising relations by visiting as leader of the Opposition in July 1971. International momentum for recognition of China became irresistible when it was announced in the same year (1971) that Kissinger had made a secret visit to China and that Nixon would visit the following year. Whitlam's visit was derided by the conservative McMahon Government, but the Kissinger announcement plus considerable pressure from conservative Australian wheat farmers worried about losing their lucrative trade to Canadian rivals, were pivotal factors in Australia's acceptance of the new realities. The decision to recognise Communist China as the legitimate China was, nonetheless, a substantial turning point in Canberra and Australia was among the first band of countries to formally recognise the PRC as the legitimate China.[14]

Successive Australian Prime Ministers after Whitlam have maintained China as a priority bilateral relationship and pursued a range of initiatives to enhance bilateral ties. Fraser shared China's view that the Soviet Union was an aggressor and subsequently received a very warm reception during his visit to Beijing in 1976. Hawke actively pursued closer ties with China and embarked on a China Action plan in the mid-1980s to develop the economic and cultural dimensions of the relationship. Keating de-linked human rights and trade after Tiananmen and Howard actively promoted China as a good international citizen and important player in the global economy.[15] Trade relations however were not significant until the mid-1990s. The last decade in particular, has witnessed an enormous shift as China's economy has continued to grow by a staggering ten percent each year. In more recent years China's growth rate has reduced somewhat but remains healthy. At the time of writing however, there were concerns about a contraction in the Chinese economy and its implications for the health of the Australian economy. The enormous demand for raw resources has placed Australia in an ideal position to ride the 'China wave' as part of its own resources boom (much like the resources boom of the 1970s with Japan's economic miracle) though there are signs that this may now be in decline somewhat.[16]

The rapid rise of China as Australia's leading trading partner highlights the seriousness of the changes taking place. A dominant issue in Canberra (and Tokyo) has been the spectacular rise of China as a global power and subsequent geo-political implications for the region. The scale of the economic rise of China has had global reverberations. Australia, as is the case with many other countries, has experienced an extraordinary change in trading patterns with China over the past decade. In 2008, for example, China just managed to surpass Japan as Australia's major trading partner. Yet only six years later (2013-14), two-way merchandise trade between Australia and China ($142.139 billion) was more than double the volume of trade Australia's enjoyed with Japan ($67,466 billion) and greater that the combined Japan and United States two –way trade with Australia ($108.087 billion).[17] Indeed the enormous boost in exports of Australian commodities to China has allowed Australia to avoid the worst of the Global Financial Crisis and maintain a relatively strong economy.

At the governmental level, the development of a 'Strategic Partnership' with China as a result of Prime Minister Gillard's visit to China in April, 2013 and the release of the White Defence paper in the same year are enlightening. The Prime Ministerial visit was highly productive and a range of agreements was reached that placed Australia in a position enjoyed by few countries. In particular, there was agreement to establish an annual leaders' meeting and ministerial dialogue with the new Chinese leadership team and to allow direct trading between the Australian dollar and the Chinese Renminbi. As well, the visit resulted in a range of important innovative agree-

ments such as the decision to embark on joint aid programs in the Asia
Pacific and to upgrade bilateral defence links. [18] Notably, efforts to achieve
these substantial milestones represented several years of negotiations. The
2013 Defence White paper, which changed the official Australian strategic
view of China from that of a 'potential threat' (2009 Defence White paper) to
'strategic partner', is part of a clear endorsement of China within government
circles and a reflection of awareness of China's importance to Australia's
national interests in decision-making circles. The signing of a Free Trade
Agreement in July 2014 and ratified by the Australian Parliament on June 17,
2015 and subsequent jubilation about the significance of the deal for the
Australian economy including massive tariffs cuts and trade worth billions of
dollars to Australian agricultural and primary producers, further highlights
the importance of the economic relationship with China. [19]

Public opinion, moreover, has changed significantly in light of the China's increased role. Surveys conducted by the Australian National University
in 2014 for example, revealed a significant shift. For the first time public
opinions was evenly divided on whether the USA (21%) or China (22%) was
more important to Australia's foreign relations. Notably 35% of those polled
believed China and the USA were of equal importance. [20]

While officially the Australian Government position has been to welcome
the rise of China, the geo-political and economic changes that have occurred
and are still taking place, have presented a range of conundrums for Australian governments: balancing triads; dealing with tension between Japan and
China on historical and territorial issues; and the reconfiguration of Australian regional diplomacy.

THREE COMPETING TRIADS

Notably triangularity—not bilateralism—and, in particular, three triads—
Australia, Japan and the United States, Australia, Japan and China and Australia, United States and China —have dominated policy planning in Australia. The focus on triangularity has important implications as it indicates a
shift from an emphasis on bilateralism (at least in regard to Japan) in Canberra. A trilateral approach represents a response to, and recognition of, the
spectacular rise of China as a major economic power and the upgraded security relationship with the United States and Japan. In all three triangles Australia, in terms of its capacity to influence, is the weakest partner and the
Australia–Japan relationship (due to Australia's relatively weak power status) is the weakest link. From an Australian perspective, the shift towards
assessing relations within a triangular context means the tendency by Australian officials to concentrate on the United States and China and to view Japan
within the prism of Sino-United States strategic competition.

Finding the appropriate range of policies towards China poses a range of interrelated problems for Australia's foreign relations with Japan. At the regional level, the difficulty is finding the balance between security and commercial interests. Both Australia and Japan have a burgeoning trade relationship with China and have made efforts to further expand commercial links in China through investment and trade opportunities. Yet as already demonstrated, Canberra and Tokyo have substantially strengthened security links and have maintained a strong commitment to an enhanced security alliance with the United States. Australia's dual strategy of close ties with the United States and proactive foreign policy becomes problematic in light of ongoing strategic competition between China and the United States and the decision in Washington to pivot in Asia.

In this context the strong relationship with Japan has serious implications for Australia's bilateral relations with China and regional diplomacy. Relations between Japan and China that involve historical animosity, a war legacy, regional rivalry and economic competition present an on-going dilemma for Australian diplomats. Close ties with Japan and burgeoning trade links and enhanced political ties with China have required skillful diplomacy by senior Australian diplomats to ensure relations are managed without directly taking sides. So far, the Australian policy approach of developing relations with China at the bilateral level has been successful. However, Chinese sensitivities on regional issues and regional leadership ambitions have the potential to dramatically change the dynamics of the relationship with Canberra. The on-going territorial dispute over the Daioyu/Senkaku Islands is a case in point. Inflamed passions and increased levels of nationalism on both sides present a range of problems for Australian officials. So far, the Australian response has been to remain neutral to avoid taking sides. However, the United States on-going support for Japan includes the Senkaku Islands as part of security treaty provisions. A serious flare-up over the islands between China and Japan has the potential to disrupt Australia's careful balancing act of improving relations with China while simultaneously maintaining and upgrading the alliance with the United States. As demonstrated by Foreign Minister Julia Bishop's criticism of the Chinese imposed Air Identification Air Defence Zone in late November 2013 and subsequent rebuke by China, Australia has to take care balancing bilateral relations. The strong condemnation by China's Foreign Minister Yang Li in face-to-face meeting in Beijing with Minister Bishop in early December 2013 was clear evidence of China's displeasure. Indeed the language used was emphatic 'Australia has jeopardised bilateral mutual trust and affected the sound growth of bilateral relations'.[21] The subsequent response by Australia to tone down criticism of Chinese policy is indicative of Australia's diplomatic dilemma and perhaps a new government 'finding its feet' in in the art of diplomacy. Notably the

April 2014 visit to China led by Prime Minister Abbott was the largest delegation ever sent by Australia to China.

In any event, enhanced Australian politico-security discussions with China such as the annual prime ministerial talks in 2014, may present more difficulties for Australia's security alignment with Japan and the United States. In particular, the decision to upgrade relations with China has important implications for the bilateral relationship with Japan. It should not be assumed in Japan, for example, that Australia is a 'natural ally' and support Japanese interests in regional forums such as the ASEAN Regional Forum or the EAC. At the third Australia–Japan conference held in February 2005 in Melbourne, the Chair report included the statement that there was a need to manage 'the emergence of China as a key player' and 'support for Japan's bid for permanent membership of the UN Security Council' (DFAT 2005). The report's recommendation implied that Australia and Japan would or should coordinate a planned response to the growing economic and political power of China. The suggestion that China should be 'managed' suggests that Australia and Japan are working in concert. A powerful pro-China lobby in Australian business circles fuelled by China's growing global position, highly lucrative trade deals and an FTA, suggests, in fact, that Australia will not always be in accord with Japan's policy.

IMPLICATIONS FOR AUSTRALIAN REGIONAL DIPLOMACY

The current on-going debate within Australia is whether a hedging strategy towards China (engaging with China while also balancing China) can be maintained. Australian diplomacy has been premised on the continuation of the established regional order that allows Australia to be proactive in the pursuit of middle power diplomacy backed by the US military alliance. The recent upgrading of bilateral relations between Australia and China highlights the challenge of maintaining a hedging strategy towards China. Australia has made the decision to develop a genuine strategic partnership with China within the next few years. The decision has led to almost unprecedented and at times fiery public debates among academics and defence specialists. In many respects, the debate is symbolic of the China question; can the current hedging strategy continue to work? Should Australia develop closer ties with China at the expense of relations with the United States and Japan? Does Australia have to make a choice?

The concern that Australia has to make a choice is encapsulated by the Hugh White's 'China Choice' thesis. According to White, the primacy of the US—led world order is under challenge by the rise of China that will have major global and regional strategic implications. His view is premised on the expectation that China will continue to maintain its phenomenal economic growth and will develop commensurate political and military power in the coming decade.[22] According to these projections; China will overtake the US as the world's largest economy by 2020. In essence, White argues that the United States has three choices in its response to China: 1. Compete; 2. Share power; or 3. Concede. His analysis is that it is in the best interest of the United States to compromise and share power with the PRC in a regional context. However the option of strategic competition is the most likely scenario. A critical issue, according to White, is that the US hedging strategy of the past 15 years – to accept and accommodate China's growing power as long as it does not threaten US primacy – can no longer be sustained. The new realities, in effect, mean that the strategic choices for Australia are limited. Already there has been a considerable shift in the region to accommodate China and the changing dynamic nature in the region (the rise of Indonesia for example) will mean that Australia must develop new strategies.[23] White's view is reinforced by his concerns that Australia is considering a full security treaty with Japan. His contention is that such an alignment is fraught with danger given current animosity between Japan and China and that the treaty would be seen in the light of Japan's efforts to contain China, thereby compromising Australia's relationship with Beijing.[24] White has also argued that Australia now faces the prospect of being a 'powerless shuttlecock' in the strategic game between Beijing and Washington. He views the recent upgrading of the relationship with China as part of the struggle between the two superpowers, with Australia oblivious to the consequences.[25] White moreover, argues that the strong support for Abe and increased military/security ties with Japan escalates rivalry between China and Japan and thereby forces to Australia to sides.[26]

Two Former Prime Ministers have weighed into this debate. Malcolm Fraser, who has recanted on his previously strong support for the United States, has argued in his book 'Dangerous Allies' that Australia should be wary of following the United States and be aware of the dangers of a potential hot war between China and Japan over territorial disputes. His central concern is to argue that Australia should become truly independent and stay out of a conflict between China and a US-backed Japan over the disputed territories.[27] Paul Keating in his Murdoch Speech in November 2012, although referring to the importance of relationships in Southeast Asia (and primarily Indonesia) made note of the need for Australia to move away from traditional allies and that Australia's sphere of influence is diminishing as a result of being too close to Washington.[28] The need have some distance from the United States has also been conveyed more generally by former senior diplomats Stuart Harris and John McCarthy. Both argue in separate papers that the relationship is too close. McCarthy contends that Canberra should reconsider its disproportionately strong security ties with the United States.[29]

Critics of Hugh White argue that although there is evidence of increasing tensions between China and the United States, the status quo in the region has not yet fundamentally changed. Australia's strategy, moreover, has been effective, though at times problematic due to the diplomatic resources required to maintain the delicate balance between the two superpowers. The notion of a 'zero sum game' in which Australia must choose between its security partner (United States) and its leading economic partner (China) is viewed as unhelpful. Security specialists Paul Dibb and Peter Jennings in separate articles argue that White has exaggerated the dangers in tensions between the two powers, overstated China's military capabilities and ignored that fact that most countries in Asia are aligning themselves with the United States. [30] Nick Bisley argues that a better economic relationship with China does not necessarily mean 'worse security relations with the United States, though he does concede that the uncertainty surrounding China's response to the United States and potential regional instability makes current policy difficult to manage. [31] And You Ji views the focus on a looming show down and the need to make a choice as a reflection of Australia's hard strategic culture rather than the current realities. He considers that the emphasis on the United States for the security of the nation has created a mindset that sets key benchmarks when assessing the strategic landscape. In this context, according to You Ji, the timing of the 2009 Defence White paper, which viewed China as a potential threat to regional stability when bilateral trade was booming and lifted Australia out of a potential recession, was an absurd situation. Indeed he noted that the view in China was that the Defence White Paper was in essence "Canberra scapegoating China in order to please the US." [32]

The perception of how we view China's rise is a core issue explored extensively by John Lee. He contends that the 'no alternative for a rising power but to compete within the existing open and liberal order argument' is too simplistic. Efforts to contain China through the 'responsible stakeholder approach', therefore, do not take into account that fact that rising powers "can seek to gradually dismantle and redesign the current order from within." [33] His argument centres on the assumption that the United States has not lost its pre-eminent strategic position and that China in fact lacks strategic leverage. In this context and given the uncertainty surrounding China, Lee contends that it is prudent for Australia to maintain its hedging strategy. [34]

Finally William T. Tow advocates that Australia has a strategic role to play in the current context that can be beneficial for regional security. He contends that it is important for Australia to continue to pursue its dual strategy of refining key security commitments to Japanese and American allies while also maintaining open and vigorous economic and political relations with China. Tow argues that doing so will provide sufficient breathing space to allow the United States and Japan to follow the Australian example in cultivating stronger security with the Chinese.[35]

The above debates reflect a period of intense debate in Australia. The increasing economic dependency on China for Australia's economic wellbeing at a time of strategic uncertainty and a question mark remains over the US pivot to Asia highlights and explains the level of discord evident. Commercial stakeholders in Australia desire that the government foster closer ties with China and argue that the economic benefits of the FTA with China supports their position. The decision in March 2015 in Canberra to be a founding member of the Asian Infrastructure Investment Bank (AIIB) despite both the United States and Japan refusing to join is a case in point. China's role in constructing the AIIB has been viewed in Washington and Tokyo as part of a strategy to construct alternative regional architecture and a possible rival to the World Bank.[36] Notably Japan has responded to the AIIB with the announcement of a 110 Billion dollar plan to boost infrastructure funding in the region through the Japan led Asia Development Bank over the next five years.[37] For Australia this has created a diplomatic dilemma; support for China's leading role in infrastructure development or the Japanese initiative with strong United States backing. The Japan Times Opinion section commented on founding members of the AIIB and noted that Australian membership was a certainty given that 40% of coal and national gas exports from Australia go to China.[38] This commentary from an opinion piece in a leading Japanese newspaper reflects tension between China and Japan over rival infrastructure banks and importantly how Australia is perceived. The expectation that Australia was a 'certainty' to join due to the heavy trade cycle with China gives insight into concerns within Japan about Australia's growing dependency on China.

The security community in Australia on the other hand is supportive of strong ties with the United States and Japan. As well as the US marine training base in Darwin, Australia's Defence Minister Kevin Andrews at the 2015 Shangri-La Dialogue in Singapore gave strong support to the United States request that China to desist in making land claims in the South China Sea. Although neutral on the territorial dispute itself, Australia has been vocal on the construction of bases and land claims by China in the disputed waters and argues that China should wait until the territorial despite is resolved.[39]

CONCLUSION

This chapter offers an Australian perspective on future directions in Australian relations with Japan and China. An attempt has been made to identify issues that will have a bearing on the bilateral relationship at the national level over the next five years and beyond. There is no likelihood of a substantial rupture or change in relations in the short-term. The continuation of a stable, close and dynamic relationship with Japan and a rapidly developing relationship with China in the mid to long-term, however, will be dependent on a range of variables that may be outside the control of policy makers in Canberra. Of particular importance is how the United States and China manage their bilateral relationship. The APEC summit meeting between Chinese President Xi Jinping and United States President Obama in the Beijing in November 2014 showcased that both cooperation (climate change) and strategic competition will be an on-going feature of bilateral relations.

Moreover, a more assertive and nationalistic China and a Abe-led LDP-Komeito Government in Japan that wishes to revise the constitution, has profound implications for regional stability and may also create a new range of problems for Canberra. In this context Australia's bilateral relationship with Japan will be increasingly affected by Canberra's rapidly improving relations with China. Australian officials have, so far, demonstrated extraordinary skill in avoiding entanglements between China and Japan and in ensuring relations with Japan are not soured by the rapidly improving relationship with China. In the mid to long-term (over the next decade), it is unlikely that Australian officials will be able to maintain this stance without risking further straining the bilateral relationship with Japan. Australian regional policies and overall foreign policy will be sorely tested. There is no compelling argument, however, why Japan should not remain a key strategic partner that encompasses both economic and security endeavours. The massive trade links, rapidly developing security ties, US alliance and shared values as stated by a succession of Prime Ministers in both countries suggest that this will be the case. The task of strengthening Australia–Japan ties is directly related to the successful broadening of what is already extensive cooperation between the two countries. In particular, the promotion of transparent multilateral dialogue on security issues that include China and the consolidation of trade liberalisation talks are of paramount importance. Various 'soft power' linkages in higher education and media exchanges remain areas in need of attention. These are ongoing issues that will shape the context of future trilateral ties between Australia, Japan and China.

The above issues reflect a general pattern in the bilateral relationship that will have a bearing on the future direction of Australia's overall foreign policy and geopolitics. How that pattern evolves will, in turn, have a substantial effect on how successful Australia will be in projecting regional influence throughout Asia. Current policies, which include a genuine engagement with China while maintaining a close security alliance with the United States and developing closer security ties with Japan, suggest that Australia, like most countries in the Asia Pacific will be pursuing a hedging strategy for the foreseeable future.

NOTES

1. For an extensive range of literature on this topic see the work of Professor Peter Drysdale, Australia-Japan Research Centre, Australian National University.
2. For detailed information see David Walton, Australia, Japan and the Region: Early Initiatives in regional diplomacy, 1952–1965 (Nova Publishers; New York, 2012).
3. Joint Declaration on Security Cooperation DFAT, March 13, 2007http://www.dfat.gov.au/geo/japan/aus_jap_security_dec.html (accessed April 10, 2007)
4. See William T.Tow, 'Tangled Webs: Security Architectures in Asia' and Malcolm Cook and Thomas Wilkins, 'The Quiet Achiever': Australia-Japan Security Relations'
5. DoD media release, Successful 2+2 Australia – Japan Meeting of Defence and Foreign Ministers', May 19, 2010. http://www.minister.defence.gov.au/2010/050.doc (accessed 6 November 2011)
6. Malcolm Cook and Thomas Wilkins, The Quiet Achiever: Australia-Japan Security Relations
7. Japan's Defence Guidelines, December 22, 2010 www.mod.go.jp/e/d_act/d_policy/pdf/summaryFY2011.pdf (accessed January 10, 2011)
8. Eiichi Katahara, Japan –Australia Joint Security Statements and the Trilateral Strategic Dialogue:
9. http://www.minister.defence.gov.au/2013/06/02/minister-for-defence- japanese-minister-of-defence-and-us-department-of-defence-joint- statement-australia-japan-united-states-defence-leaders-trilateral- meeting-joint-statement/ (accessed June 14, 2013)
10. See Yusuke Ishida, 'Japan-Australia Security Relations and the Rise of China: Pursuing the Bilateral-Plus Approaches' UNISCI Discussion Papers no.32 May 2013. Ryo Sahashi also views the Australia-Japan relationship as a critical element of a more complex web of security arrangements. See Sahashi Security Arrangements in the Asia Pacific: A Three Tier Approach in William T. Tow and Rikki Kersten eds. Bilateral Perspectives on Regional Security: Australia, Japan and the Asia Pacific Region (Palgrave MacMillan; New York; 2012).
11. See Visit to Japan by the Hon. Tony Abbott, Prime Minister of the Commonwealth of Australia, April 5 to 8, 2014http://www.mofa.go.jp/a_o/ocn/au/page3e_000160.html (cited April 12, 2014).
12. Australia and Japan to jointly develop defence technology' http://www.straitstimes.com/the-big-story/asia- report/japan/story/japan-australia-jointly-develop-defence-equipment-20140612 (accessed July 10, 2014).
13. David Wroe, Sydney Morning Herald, May 24, 2015 http://www.smh.com.au/world/foreign-minister-julie-bishop-and-prime-minister-shinzo-abe-strike-military-deal-20150523-gh85t0.html (cited June 20, 2015)
14. The Whitlam Institute located at the University of Western Sydney has released an extensive collection of material on this matter. The web site is http://www.whitlam.org/gough_whitlam/china (cited June 13, 2013). For more information on debates within Australia about recognition of China see Edmund Fung and Colin Mackerras, *From Fear to Friendship: Australia's foreign policy towards China 1968 to 1982* (University of Queensland Press; St Lucia, 1985) and James Curran, 'The World Changes: Australia's China Policy in the Wake of Empire' in James Reilly and Jingdong Yuan eds. Australia and China at 40 New South Publishing, Sydney, 2012 pp. 22-43.
15. For a good overview of issues in the bilateral relationship see Nicolas Thomas (ed.), *Reorientating Australia-China Relations: 1972 to the Present* (Ashgate; Aldershot, 2004).
16. World Bank economic figures for China have indicated a gradual slowing of the economy due to economic transition. Economic growth in 2013 (7.7%), 2014 (7.7%) and the World Bank forecast for 2015 (7.5%) are indicative of a slight decline in overall economic growth in China. See http://www.worldbank.org/en/country/china/publication/china-economic-update-june-2014 For Australian coverage of a possible downturn in the Chinese economy and its implications for Australia see Paul Kelly 'Hold on tight, our economy is heading for the biggest of falls' http://www.theaustralian.com.au/opinion/columnists/hold-on-tight-our-economy-is-heading-for-the-biggest-of-falls/story-e6frg74x-1226630292612 (accessed June 22, 2013).

17. See Department of Foreign Affairs and Trade fact sheets on China http://www.dfat.gov.au/geo/fs/chin.pdf Japan http://www.dfat.gov.au/geo/fs/japan.pdf and fact sheet on the United States http://www.dfat.gov.au/geo/fs/usa.pdf (accessed January 18, 2015). I added the figures for Australia's two-way merchandise trade with Japan and United States.

18. Prime Ministers Homepage http://www.pm.gov.au/press-office/prime-minister-gillard-concludes-visit-china (accessed June 6, 2013)

19. http://dfat.gov.au/trade/agreements/Pages/benefits-of-ftas.aspx (accessed June 21, 2015)

20. http://politicsir.cass.anu.edu.au/sites/default/files/ANUpoll_Foreign_policy.pdf   (accessed September 1, 2014)

21. East China Sea row escalates as Yang Yi tells Julia Bishop Australia has jeopardised trust,   http://www.abc.net.au/news/2013-12-07/east-sea-dispute-between-china-and-australia-escalates/5142080 (accessed December 10, 2013).

22. Hugh White, ' China Choice'

23. Hugh White, 'China Choice'

24. Hugh White, 'Right now we do not need an alliance with Japan'

25. Hugh White, ' Australia is now a pawn in US-China power play'

26. Hugh White, Strategic Insights ASPI, August 2014

27. Malcolm Fraser and Cain Roberts, *Dangerous Allies*, (Melbourne University Press, Melbourne 2014).

28. Paul Keating, The Keith Murdoch Oration 'Asia in the New Order

29. John McCarthy, Australia and the US – Too close for comfort? http://www.internationalaffairs.org.au/australian_outlook/australia-the-united-states-and-asia/   (accessed May 14, 2015).

30. Paul Dibb, 'Why I disagree with Hugh White' and Paul Jennings, ASPI Strategic Insight, August 2014

31. See Nick Bisley, 'Never having to choose'

32. You Ji, 'Managing offbalance tripartite relations'

33. John Lee, 'Divergence in Australia's Economic and Security interests?'

34. Lee, Divergence in Australia's Economic and Security Interests? P. 161

35. William. T. Tow ' How Australia-Japan Relations 'Fit' into Security Dynamics'

36. http://www.theguardian.com/business/2015/mar/29/australia-confirms-it-will-join-chinas-asian-infrastructure-investment-bank (accessed June 21, 2015)

37. http://thediplomat.com/2015/05/is-this-japans-new-challenge-to-chinas-infrastructure-bank/ (accessed May 23, 2015)

38. http://www.japantimes.co.jp/opinion/2015/04/20/commentary/japan-commentary/japan-wont-join-aiib/#.VYZ7blWqqko (cited May 30, 2015)

39. ww.minister.defence.gov.au/2015/05/31/minister-for-defence-114th-iiss-asia-security-summit-the-shangri-la-dialogue-singapore/ (cited June 18, 2015)

Chapter Six

Are There Normative Powers in the Asia-Pacific?

An Inquiry into the Normative Power of China and Japan[1]

Emilian Kavalski, Associate Professor, Australian Catholic University

It is often overlooked that World War II marked not only a major change in the dynamics of global politics, but that it also indicated a qualitative shift in the way such patterns were observed. Namely, "the study of international politics replaced the study of international organizations as the guiding concern and the fundamental point of reference in international relations; [the focus] had turned to the study of underlying forces and trends which shape and mold the behavior of all nation states."[2] In this respect, the contention has been that it was the very post-World War II setting that allowed the discipline of International Relations (IR) to grow "more self-conscious and academically assured."[3] This tendency, however, has been greatly assisted by the growing "apple pie"[4] flavor of IR as a result of the superpower status of the USA during the Cold War period and the concomitant preponderance (and consequent globalization) of the English language as the *lingua franca* of (not only American) diplomacy and academia. Thus, while the key terms of the discipline—sovereignty, nationalism, balance of power, etc.—have their roots in the history of European affairs, the analysis of world politics during the post-World War II period gradually became "an American social science."[5]

Thus, when commentators have recently started to note that there is "no non-Western IR theory" to account for the alleged "power shift to the East" in global politics,[6] what they have in mind is that there is precious little in the IR mainstream which is neither intimately related to the narratives of "American IR," nor originates (either conceptually or in practice) in the context of Washington's Cold War concerns. In an attempt to challenge these biases, this chapter draws attention to the growing significance of (if not necessarily contestation between) normative powers in Asia. Despite its centrality to European IR theory (probably, the most prominent non-American IR school to emerge in the wake of the Cold War), the notion of normative power has had surprisingly little traction in the analysis of the nascent agency of international actors other than the European Union (EU)—especially, the explanation and understanding of the outreach of Asian actors such as China and Japan. There are several reasons for this development. On the one hand, owing to the perceived complexity of the EU, Asian scholars have been disinterested to engage with the propositions and concepts of European IR. On the other hand, European IR scholars have expanded little effort to translate the applicability of their terminology to non-EU actors and contexts (both because of the all-pervasive nature of the EU and also because of the positioning of Asian Studies outside of the IR curriculum). At the same time (and probably most significantly), both European and Asian IR scholars have tended to frame their analysis in reaction to (yet, in conversation with) the dominant American IR view, which—instead of aiding—appears to have further deepened the rift, by hampering their engagement with one another.[7]

In an attempt to redress this trend, this chapter takes as its point of departure the suggestion that we are witnessing a "rise of normative powers" in global life. Such an assertion might sound like a misnomer to some. To begin with, it can be argued that the behavior of all international actors—whether they be states, international organizations, or non-state actors—is embedded in certain rules, standards, and principles of behavior. As Hans Morgenthau has discerned "all nations are tempted—and few have been able to resist the temptation for long—to clothe their own particular aspirations and actions in the moral purposes of the universe."[8] While not everyone need agree with the significance of this normativity to the agency of particular actors, it nevertheless indicates certain value-based judgment underpinning their international interactions. Yet, the suggestion here is much more straightforward—just because any international behavior can be labeled as normative should not lead one to assume that in fact all actors are normative powers (even if some of their actions have normative side effects).

On the contrary, following Ian Manners' oft-quoted definition, normative powers are only those actors that can "shape what can be 'normal' in international life." As he insists (and few would disagree) "the ability to define what passes for 'normal' in world politics is, ultimately, the greatest power of all."[9] In a similar fashion, Jay Jackson (nearly three decades earlier, but in a different context) defined "normative power" as "the potential for influencing activity… [through] the power of norms," which outlines the "*domain and range*" of legitimate behavior.[10] In this respect, both Jackson and Manners intuit that the reference to normative power suggests an ability to frame what is acceptable and what is unacceptable behavior. However, while Manners tends to prioritize the *ability* of an actor to define the "normal," Jackson stresses the *legitimacy* of the definitions of the "normal" – i.e., this legitimacy needs to be earned.[11]

It needs to be stressed at the outset that the notion of normative power is quite distinct from Joseph Nye's oft-quoted understanding of "soft power," which is often presented as its conceptual sibling. Nye defines soft power as "getting others to want the outcomes that you want."[12] While many will argue that the notions of soft power and normative power are twin-concepts, the claim here is that the ramification of the normal implies a much more comprehensive leadership in international life than merely getting others to want the same outcomes as you. In fact, normative power is about demonstrating palpable constitutive effects, which go beyond the mere co-optation and shaping the preferences of other actors emphasized in the definition of soft power.[13] Instead, others do not perceive to be following somebody else's goals, but their own. This is what defining the ramifications of the normal entails—it alters the perceptions and attitudes of target states, so that they internalize the perspectives of the normative power in their daily practices. Thus, the positioning of an actor as a normative power—even if such positioning is a product of self-construction—can have a significant bearing on that actor's socializing capacities and ability to influence the international identities of its counterparts.[14]

And it is in the contest over legitimacy that the significance of the rise of normative powers emerges. In other words, while this offers a conceptual outline of the workings of normative power in Asia (by examining the examples provided by China, and Japan), recent analyses have suggested a much wider proliferation of normative agency in global life—for instance, in reference to the external outreach of Brazil,[15] India,[16] Turkey,[17] Russia,[18] ASEAN,[19] etc. It could be argued that such broadening in the scope of the normative power research agenda offers a mere reflection of the growing exposure of scholars to the ratiocination of European IR. However, such an explanation provides only a lopsided and superfluous account of the qualitative changes underpinning the growing interest in normative agency. A more detailed probing of this trend will reveal that owing to the lack of clarity on "who the leading power [in international relations] will be, nor what its intentions will be"[20] has ushered in a palpable leadership vacuum, which has assisted the normative entrepreneurship of various international actors. Thus, going back to the context of Asia, the proposition of a rise of normative powers suggests that actors such as the EU, China, and Japan proffer themselves as exemplars of distinct patterns of international interactions. The models they project are framed by their idiosyncratic strategic cultures which inform not only the cognitive frameworks of their international interactions, but also the way(s) in which they practice policy-making. Thus, the expression of what is 'normal' invokes certain agenda and entails power relations. Yet, what distinguishes normative power from other types of power is how these relations of asymmetry are managed. On an instrumental level, normative power is "neither military, nor purely economic, but one that works through ideas and opinions."[21] Substantively, however, normative powers are "other empowering."[22] In other words, normative power reflects a particular quality not just of leadership in international relations, but of the very nature of power in world affairs—namely, that it is contextually contingent and depends on social recognition within a community.[23] In this respect, normative power reflects "an actor's ability to present his own particular worldview as compatible with the communal aims."[24]

This brings us back to Jackson's definition and his insistence that *tolerance* is a key aspect of normative power. As tolerant international actors, normative powers are characterized by "a willingness to suspend evaluation of others' activity," which then triggers a specific set of "expectations by others for [a normative] actor's conduct."[25] Thus, unlike the relationships of great powers (or even soft powers for that matter), those of normative powers—by their very nature—are dialogical. In particular, as it will be explained shortly, the recognition of a normative power is highly contingent on its relations with other actors, and these relations, by definition, cannot be dictated by the normative power alone; "it must be negotiated and mutually constituted in bilateral and multilateral contexts."[26] In this setting, Jackson's emphasis on the significance of tolerance reframes E.H. Carr's intuition that "power goes far to create the morality convenient to itself, and coercion is a fruitful source of consent. But when all these reserves have been made, it remains true that a new international order and a new international harmony can be built up only on the basis of an ascendancy which is generally accepted as tolerant and unoppressive."[27]

The reference to a rise of normative powers inscribes itself within project of decentering the study of normative power by taking it "outside of [its] Eurocentric box."[28] The claim is that non-Western normative orders are just as legitimate as Western ones.[29] This investigation therefore acknowledges the emergence of alternative (and oftentimes) contending conceptualizations of political goods in global life and the appropriate way(s) for their attainment. Thus, the contention of a rise of normative powers can be interpreted as a contemporary twist on the age-old inquiry into what a multi-polar theory of international relations might look like.[30] If one is to pursue such a study, the parallel investigation of normative powers promises to open the doors to a contextual exploration of the intellectual foundations not only of multipolarity, but also to the proliferation of a cacophony of normative languages in global life.

The claim is that the EU, China, and Japan offer some of the most conspicuous indications of the different types of normative power both in Asia and in global life. What transpires in this rise of normative powers is a "balance of practices" distinct from the conventional "balance for power."[31] Thus, the unevenness underpinning the distinct repertoires of normative power practices promoted by Brussels, Beijing, and Tokyo in different global locales emerges from the distinct logics of action informing their international agency. In other words, the positioning of an actor as a normative power is not stable or fixed, but highly fluid and, thereby, demands constant and ongoing practices for its legitimation and re-legitimation. In such a relation and contextual framing, the notion of normative power can be "best understood not in terms of its quantifiable capabilities but *within* its specific social contexts. The 'same amount' of capability may not translate into the same degree of power or achieve the same effect within different relationships or domains."[32] In this respect, one of the central claims of this article is that normative power emerges as a *power in context*—it is not entirely an intrinsic property of an actor, but depends on the kind of interactions it has in specific contexts.

The suggestion is that "any power instrument becomes a potential power resource only if its control is seen to be valued by other actors in the interaction. Power comes out of this relation, not from the power holder alone."[33] Such emphasis on the significance of context comes to suggest that what is at stake are not the perceptions or misperceptions of other actors about who is or is not a normative power, but those actors' "*subjective* expectations and understandings, both of which are strongly affected by cultural settings."[34] Thus, it is the contingent (temporal and spatial) context of each interaction— rather than an actor's perception or misperception—that encourages an actor to interpret its partner's behavior as that of a normative power or not. In other words, contexts can act as a "cause," a "barrier," and a "changing meaning"[35] for the normative power of international actors. Normative power therefore is not necessarily only about affecting the perceptions of other actors (which offers a rather limited scope of action), but mostly about framing the responses of those other actors. As Erik Ringmar cogently observes, the "reaction [of other actors] is far more important than the action itself and their reaction is what the exercise of power ultimately seeks to influence."[36]

The claim thereby is that normative power emerges *in relation to* the inter-subjective environment to which its agency is applied. Thus, the reference to a "rise of normative powers" emerges as shorthand for their "struggle for recognition." As it will be explained, an actor's capacity to define the 'normal' depends on the recognition of this agency by target states. The emphasis on recognition-in-context draws attention to the performative qualities of normative power, which intimates that *to be* a normative power is oftentimes less important than to *appear to be* a normative power. The suggested rise of normative powers in global life—such as the ones of the EU, China, and Japan—indicates their nascent contestation for such recognition. In other words, recognition becomes the permissive context for an actor's normative power. Before detailing this dynamic, the following sections briefly outline the EU's, China's, and then Japan's normative power. "Normative power Europe," "normative power China," and "normative power Japan" are treated here as ideal types. While concurring that such conceptualizations are rarely countenanced in their purest and isolated form, it is useful to surmise the ideal types to elicit the nascent struggle for recognition of normative powers in global life.

NORMATIVE POWER EUROPE: STILL A CONTRADICTION IN TERMS?

When discussing the external affairs of the EU, most commentators note its interdependent politico-economic framework flaunting the benefits of liberal democracy. Such a context informs the EU's intent to promote the establishment of transparent forms of governance, viable market mechanisms, and strong civil societies in countries around the world. These objectives are the very reason why the Brussels-based bloc has been referred to as a normative power. Its actorness—despite the hardening (even if only in rhetoric) contained in the Lisbon Treaty and identification through the civilian instruments of its soft power capabilities (aid, preferential trade agreements, institutional twinning, etc.)—is still defined by the norms and values that belie the strategic interests of the EU in global life. This understanding is implicit in the international roles of the EU—it aims to "Europeanize" the behavior of other states. Thus, and owing to the dominant focus on enlargement, the EU's normative power has been treated largely as coterminous with the transformative potential underwriting the dynamics of accession-driven conditionality. Thereby, it was only recently that the relevance of the EU's ability to alter the practices of states (outside of the purview and the prospect of membership) has been given serious consideration. It seems, however, that the bulk of popular and policy attention has been captured by the development of the European Neighborhood Policy (ENP). In this respect, the socialization processes embedded in the exercise of normative power Europe reveal clear assumptions of superiority—i.e., "it is the non-EU Europe that needs to learn to adapt," not the EU.[37] Consequently, the kind of normalization of international affairs embedded in the EU's normative power reflect its assumed privileged position. In short, others are expected to comply with the projected "European model."

As the case of the post-communist countries of Eastern Europe reveals, such compliance is introduced through the process of accession-driven socialization. It is this experience that has convinced the EU of the validity of the "logic of appropriateness" as a guide for its external strategies. Hence, it was the willing internalization of "European' identities, values, and norms by post-communist countries that made possible the normative power of the EU."[38] It is in this setting that the governance model implicit in the processes of Europeanization frames EU-accession as "the single most powerful policy instrument for peace and security in the world."[39] The articulation of normative power Europe makes explicit the securitization of the integration process by and within the strategic culture of the EU. Integration (by way of Europeanization) gains urgency and immediacy because its alternative—disintegration—seems certain to unleash unpredictable dynamics that portend the end of the project of "Europe."[40] This then leads to the prioritization of the norms and values that allow the EU to *be* a normative power, because it is these standards of behavior that frame the outlines of the "normal." In terms of Brussels' global outreach, however, the overwhelming attention to the Europeanisation of candidate states appears to have undercut the operational effectiveness of EU's normative power in "out-of-Europe" areas. This is not least, because the EU has had very little reasons (as well as time) to develop such capacities while the East European enlargement was still ongoing and, consequently, because of the preoccupation with the harmonization of the interactions among 27 Member States in the context of a protracted ratification of the Lisbon Treaty. The Eurozone debt crisis seems to offer another such "distraction" from the projection of effective normative power to "out-of-Europe" areas. As Michael Smith has eloquently argued,

> The status of the EU as a continental model of economic and social organization might be seen as giving a strong basis for the development of European foreign policy, but in many ways the strengths that give the EU a major role in the European order do not export easily; they are less immediately appropriate to a fluid and often chaotic world, and this means that the attempt to project "Europe" into the global arena brings with it new risks and potential costs.[41]

It is in this context that the contention of normative power Europe still appears as a contradiction in terms in "out-of-Europe" areas. Brussels does not seem capable of formulating relations with countries beyond the realms of membership and privileged partnership that would sustain the socializing influence of its normative power. In this respect, the cultural instincts underpinning the Europeanizing mechanisms developed for prospective candidate states and neighborhood countries appear ill-suited to the dynamic environment of most "out-of-Europe" areas. The complexity of global life confronts the EU with the reality where other countries do not perceive it as a magnet. This is a qualitatively new condition for Brussels and its normative power—a situation, which appears to baffle the EU and one, which it still has not addressed convincingly. Thus, used to the socialization of post-communist countries compliant with its normative power, the EU appears confused and uncertain by the lack of appeal of its values.[42]

In its external affairs, therefore, the EU continues to insist on the internalization of its norms by various countries around the world, however without the support of its explicit instruments for socialization, which are part and parcel of its enlargement policy. This confirms the suggestion that the ability of the EU's normative power to affect others is dependent upon its own awareness of a particular kind of self.[43] Thus, the socializing agency of the EU depends not so much on its capabilities, but on the way it constructs relationships through which its normative power is applied in different global locales. In this respect, the EU's search for a "new" external strategy (beyond enlargement and enlargement-like initiatives such as the Eastern Partnership of the ENP) demands a serious reflection upon the framework of its own normativity. Without such questioning (or what others have called "let[ting] go of its civilizational conceits")[44] the EU is unlikely to emerge as a viable normative power beyond the geographical confines of Europe and its immediate neighborhood.

NORMATIVE POWER CHINA: FRAMING HARMONIOUS RELATIONSHIPS

China's expanding outreach and diversifying roles have provided a novel context for the ongoing reconsiderations of world politics. In the wake of the Cold War, commentators were pondering how far Western ideas can/would spread in a geopolitical environment characterized by "the end of history." Today, the debate seems to be how far Chinese ideas will reach. In this setting, the focus on Beijing's fledgling normative power suggests that international affairs need to be understood not only as fractures into territorially-defined spaces, but also by social relations and their socio-cultural and eco-historical nexus of reference.[45] It has to be acknowledged from the outset that while the study of normative power China is of recent provenance,[46] the inquiry into the transformations and the transformative potential of China's foreign policy has become a virtual cottage industry in the last two decades. In particular, there is a heated debate whether China provides an "Eastphalian" "example," "model," "mode," or a "new paradigm" for the study and practice of world affairs.[47] Such assessments of the security, economic, and foreign policy implications of China's rise provide the background for the outline of normative power China offered in this section.

This distinct point of departure brings into focus the norms and values of China's foreign policy. Such consideration reflects at least three distinct readings of China's *guoqing* (national peculiarities).[48] These contextualizations gain significance because Chinese normative power might actually represent the most conspicuous indication of the "return to tradition *(huixiang chuantong)*" dominating the country's foreign policy thinking.[49] Thus, regardless of their stance, the proponents of China's normative power intimate that is informed by the long shadow of its philosophical oeuvre (especially, Confucianism, but also Daoism and the works of numerous pre-Qin thinkers). Even the Chinese Communist Party has been actively seeking to infuse Confucian principles into its Marxist underpinnings in order to increase its domestic legitimacy.[50] It is not coincidental therefore that the mushrooming of Confucius Institutes around the world has become one of the most conspicuous indications of China's global outreach. There have been two aspects to Beijing's "patriotic worrying *(youhuan)*" about China's capacity to attain the "ultimate perfection *(da tong)*" necessary for its influence to radiate outwards.[51]

On the one hand, China has been keen to learn from the experience of previous great powers. This reflects a key aspect of current Chinese international relations thinking according to which the dynamics of world politics represent a "succession of hegemonies."[52] On the other hand, the reflexivity animating China's international agency has been much more introspective and has tended to focus on China's own historical recollection. In this respect, the lessons that are gleaned are not only from the experience of other international actors, but also from the legacy of China's own past glory and decline.[53] Thus, the patterns of China's nascent normative power present an intriguing intersection of the discursive memory of the past with the contexts of the present and the anticipated tasks of the future. In particular, China's introspective look recollects a normative power premised on the practices of interaction rather than explicit norms of appropriateness.

The emphasis on dialogue has had significant implications for the evolution of China's normative power. For instance, it has promoted an understanding that a position of leadership cannot be inflicted upon others (by force or through domination), but needs to be earned (in the process of interaction). Brantley Womack argues that this attitude is crucial to understanding China's socializing propensities. He singles out "respect for the other" as the "cardinal virtue" of Beijing's normative power. Thus, by lavishing attention to countries "that normally do not get much respect," China sets itself as a different kind of actor (if not necessarily as an alternative model). Beijing's insistence on "respect for the other" becomes an important boon for its normative power:

> In a world of equals, each is in a similar situation, and each can respond in kind to the actions of others. With symmetry, respect for others can be reduced to the Golden Rule, because in fact others can do to you what you do to them.

In a world of asymmetric relationships, respect—appreciation for the situation and autonomy of the other—requires special attention. Respect for the weaker side is not simply noblesse oblige or an act of generosity of the stronger. The weaker can only afford to be deferential to the strong when they feel that their identity and boundaries will be respected.[54]

The emphasis on *respect for the other* intuits that Chinese normative power is underpinned by the principle, "let others reach their goals as you reach yours."[55] Normative power in this respect is necessarily contextual—Chinese (especially Confucian) traditions assert that definitions of the "normal" are contingent and depend on "who we are interacting with, and when."[56] The individuation implicit in the logic of relationships suggests the profound ontological implications of interactions—"the appreciation of what is important to you in terms of your own self-conception, in contrast to the general expectations that [the international] society may impose on you [provides] an increasing scope for self-realization."[57] This inference brings us back to Brantley Womack, who proposes that unlike the normative power of the EU which is framed by "logic of appropriateness," China's normative power is framed by "logic of relationships." Such logic,

assumes that while the future is unknown, the partners in the future are the same as in the past and present. Therefore, the significance of any specific interaction lies in how it shapes a particular relationship... The bottom line in a relationship logic is that both sides feel that they are better off if the relationship continues—this is the minimum meaning of "mutual benefit." A normal relationship does not require symmetry of partners or equality of exchanges, but it does require reciprocity [i.e., respect for the other].[58]

What is crucial about the understanding of normative power through such logic of relationships is that the *norms* for the normal are no longer defined by the leading state in terms of "rights and obligations," but emerge as "behavioral standards" accepted by the majority of participating states in the process of interaction.[59] The emphasis here is that Beijing's normative power engages other states in the practice of doing together—i.e., *they do as China does*. This pattern is distinct from the security governance practiced by Western actors (especially, the EU), which is premised on the conditionality of "*do as I say, not as I do*."[60]

NORMATIVE POWER JAPAN: LEADERSHIP BY EMULATION

In March 1970, *Time* magazine carried a ten-page lead story tracing the gradual, but seemingly inevitable shift in international affairs "towards the Japanese century." The century that the authors had in mind was the twenty-first century. At the time, Japan's impressive record of growth was considered nothing short of an economic miracle and likely to backstop Tokyo's resurgence on the global stage. In this context, the then Japanese Prime Minister, Eisaku Sato, articulated probably one of the earliest outlines of normative power Japan, by explicitly aspiring for: "an era when Japan's national power will carry unprecedented weight in world affairs." He suggested that Japan should be a 'content but not an arrogant' country, whose example would inspire "the whole world to agree that the human race is far richer for Japan's existence."[61]

While it remained unclear at the time whether Japan can indeed serve as a model for the rest of the world, commentators and policy-makers in Washington were taking note and becoming increasingly apprehensive about (what they perceived as) Tokyo's growing independence and entrepreneurship in global life. For instance, already in the early 1980s some were making projections that within a decade Japan would be as intransigent as Charles de Gaulle's France had been; and in fact hinted that Tokyo has merely been feigning subscription to shared values, for purely pragmatic considerations of economics and security.[62] A decade later, Joseph Nye went as far as arguing that the US needs to 'manage' actively Japan's economic superpower—and in fact "harness" it—if it were to remain the sole superpower after the collapse of the Soviet Union.[63] Echoing these sentiments the political economist Lester Thurow fretted that if Washington fails to act "we are all going to wind up working for the Japanese."[64] In this respect, it is not surprising that many were quick to label Japan as not merely a challenger to US dominance, but "the enemy" in the post-Cold War period and since the two were perceived to be on a "collision course,"[65] war between them seemed anything but inevitable.[66]

Underpinning such assessments was the concern that Tokyo will not so much seek to assert its foreign policy independence from Washington, but that Japan can become a lodestone for other countries in Asia (and the rest of the world) as an alternative model for international affairs that can severely undercut US influence and interests. In particular, what seemed to bother American commentators was the suggestion that Japan's "Asian identity" prevents it from committing whole-heartedly to "the Western international order."[67] What many found particularly disquieting was Japan's reticence to entangle itself in global human rights issues owing to concerns that it can "expose itself to unnecessary position-taking."[68] Thus, the potential for Japan to become a new kind of international actor—namely "a superpower without superweapons," which has a no-strings-attached foreign policy stance[69] —has intimated latent prospects for reframing the US/Western-set definitions of the 'normal' in international life.

Similar to China, the study of normative power Japan is of recent pedigree,[70] but it draws on the debates surrounding the outlines of a "Pax Nipponica"[71] (Vogel, 1986) and the implications from Japan's "halfway to hegemon'" status.[72] What appears to be at the heart of Japanese normative power is a commitment to responsible global citizenship in an increasingly interdependent world. In particular, both in the context of the Cold War and after, publicizing the idea that a country can meaningfully shape the dynamics of international affairs without the military means to enforce its will on others tends to be treated as a subversion to the dominant paradigms for explanation and understanding. As Marvin Soroos has long insisted, the key aspect of Japan's attempt to reframe what passes for "normal" in international life is its willingness to engage actively in the construction of a peaceful and stable world order through diplomatic initiatives, the effective engagement in international institutions, and the expansion of its foreign aid program. Thus, by setting itself as an example for "global responsibility" Japan has challenged the mantra of power politics by promoting a cooperative agenda for addressing global problems premised on a variety of "positive and associative ways in which governments can work together to improve the quality of life not only for their own populations but also for peoples of other countries; and by doing so, they also diminish markedly the risk of war."[73]

Equally importantly, the evolution of normative power Japan reflects not merely commitment to global responsibility, but responsiveness to the expectations and needs of its partners.[74] Thus, Japan's commitment to "incipient multilateralism"[75] —not least by championing the UN's human security agenda in the immediate post-Cold War period—indicated to many that the country has found a niche to exert normative power not only in Asia, but globally.[76] In particular, Japan's affiliation with the "freedom from want" aspect of human security (as opposed to the more controversial "freedom from fear" advocated by Canada during the 1990s and which became associated with various military humanitarian interventions) allowed Tokyo to build on its longstanding development-oriented projects while eschewing any overt commitment to political conditionality.[77] The intent of these activities has been to validate the credibility and legitimacy of Japan's international outreach.

In this respect, normative power Japan reveals Tokyo's 'intellectual and instrumental leadership' as well as the adaptive capacity to establish itself as an international "trouble-shooter" and a source of innovative solutions to global problems.[78] The suggestion is that Japan has been able to achieve this by "tapping into new sources of strength in order to remain a key player in Asia, just as it has many times before."[79] Yet, unlike the proactive underpinnings of both normative power Europe and normative power China, normative power Japan has been far less activist in its agency. Its normative power tends to focus on promoting and supporting international norms that are more or less already popular in the international society. In this respect, what distinguishes normative power Japan is that it aims to generate attraction by appropriating already-accepted global norms rather than promoting a particular vision of world order that would significantly challenge any established outlook or practice.[80] This is reflected both in its espousal of human security in the 1990s[81] and environmental protection in the 2000s.[82] More broadly, the evolution of normative power Japan confirms Tokyo's reluctance to take positions of leadership and take responsibility for trouble-shooting issues in reaction to international expectations.[83]

CONCLUSION: NORMATIVE POWER AND THE STRUGGLE FOR RECOGNITION

The parallel assessment of the normative powers of the EU, China, and Japan draws attention to one of the crucial aspects of world affairs—the feature that the basic ontological condition of international actors is relational (i.e., the content of their existence as actors is constituted inter-subjectively during the process of interaction).[84] The contention here is that contemporary world affairs are not merely about who gets what, when, and how (if they ever really were), but also about how nascent normative powers engage other actors. In this setting, normative powers need to be perceived as legitimate— i.e., their agency depends on the validation by target actors (usually through different types of compliance or conformity). The EU, China, and Japan are motivated by a *desire to be recognized* as actors that are not only capable, but who also have the right to set the ramifications of the "normal" in global life. This is a reminder that power itself is not an attribute of an actor, but a relationship in which "nothing remains fixed, neither the old basic institutions and systems of rules nor the specific organizational forms and roles of the actors; instead, they are disrupted, reformulated, and renegotiation during the course of interaction itself."[85] Normative powers, therefore, should be perceived as neither the "goodies" nor the "baddies" of global life. Instead, as the analyses of the EU, China, and Japan have demonstrated, they are merely *powers*. In this respect, the contextual effectiveness of normative power is a product of design, rather than chance (let alone osmosis).

Thus, Brussels, Beijing, and Tokyo are learning that for their normative power to be considered legitimate, they themselves are expected to behave in certain ways to earn such recognition. In other words, the viability of either the "EU model," the "China model," and the "Japan model" is not entirely dependent either on Brussels', on Beijing's, or on Tokyo's decisions, but contingent on the interpretation of their agency by other actors. In this setting, *recognition* emerges as "the core constitutive moment" of international interactions and refers to "the communicative process in the international society of states through which states mutually acknowledge the status and social esteem of other states."[86] The acknowledgement of this nascent struggle for recognition suggests that the contestation between normative powers moves beyond their relative capability—i.e., it cannot be captured through the narratives of 'struggle for power'. In other words, the answer to the question "Who or what exists politically as a normative power?" is "Those actors that are *recognized* as normative powers." Recognition, in this setting, is indicated by the specific attitudes, dispositions, and behavior of target states. This then raises the question: "Under what conditions are target states willing to grant such recognition?" The answer provided in this study is that normative powers are granted recognition when they deliver credible commitments to the intended target. In other words, defining the "normal" in international life is "essentially a collective enterprise: the ongoing if subtle interplay, between common needs and norms, and a [normative power's] capacity to understand and respond to those collective aspirations."[87]

In this respect, the pattern (and perception) of international anarchy is animated by the "status insecurity" of actors.[88] Such status insecurity stems from the uncertainty associated with the inter-subjective constitution of identity in global life. Ultimately, all actors in international life have the fundamental autonomy to follow or not to follow someone's lead. Thus, the diverse tools used to signal recognition or disrespect provide means for validating or casting doubt on other actor's narratives about themselves.[89] Recognition is both tentative and revocable,[90] which attests to the "constitutive vulnerability" of international actors—especially, normative powers—"to the unpredictable reactions and responses of others."[91] This further accentuates the contextual nature of normative power—its agency "must fit the needs and aspirations of its followers;" otherwise a normative power risks losing its followers not because it has changed, but because the pattern of wants and desires of its followers has.[92]

The struggle for recognition among normative powers is not merely "a part of," but becomes constitutive of the complex systemic logic of global life.[93] To put it bluntly, normative powers perform particular roles on the international stage and were they not to follow the (script of those) expectations, normative powers would no longer be acknowledged as such. As Headley Bull has presciently noticed in the post-World War II international affairs, great powers need to be "*recognized* by others to have certain special rights and duties."[94] Likewise, his fellow Cold War IR theorist, Hans Morgenthau has asserted the significance of recognition in his avowal that the "prestige of a nation is its reputation for power. That reputation, the reflection of the reality of power in the mind of the observers can be as important as the reality of power itself. *What others think about us is as important as what we actually are.*"[95] The legitimacy of normative power thereby derives from and is embedded in the practices through which it projects its social purpose in global life. As Ian Clark perceptively notes,

[international affairs] is always a contested normative space, and this is en-
demic in its nature, rather than simply the result of failure of any one attempt
to overcome it. In such a contested space, all powerful actors have to earn their
varying degrees of respect and legitimacy, and are unable to command it at
will. This very unruliness underscores the pluralistic character of international
society and paradoxically makes the business of its practices of legitimacy all
the more serious and arduous: it is the reason also why legitimacy matters so
much, rather than any reason to dismiss it as irrelevant.[96]

Thus, the recognition *by* others rests on recognition *of* others. In this
context, the reference to normative power indicates an actor's ability to show
consideration for the effects of its actions on others—namely, a normative
power retains its status to the extent that it meets the expectations of its
followers.[97] The ability to treat others with respect allows normative powers
to gain the recognition that creates the permissive environment allowing
them to define and redefine the standards of the "normal" in international
life. Thus, the international identity of an actor is not just about capabilities,
but mostly about recognition—which is both an outcome and a reassertion of
an actor's normative power. Status is therefore contingent upon the inter-
subjective construction of identity, which "is not (only) threatened by others,
but also possible because of them [as] they are always already involved *in*
[an actor's] identity."[98] Consequently, anarchy is not just "what states make
of it," but what reaction actors engender in their struggle for recognition. By
outlining the normative power of the EU, China, and Japan, this analysis has
indicated the nascent rise of normative powers—international actors demanding recognition for their ability to define the ramifications of the "normal" in global life.

As it has been outlined in the preceding sections (i) the EU has elaborated
a rule-based model of normative power, (ii) China has developed a relation-
ship-based one, (iii) while Japan favors a leadership pattern premised on
responsiveness to the needs of its partners. Since social life never ceases its
interactive dynamics and keeps on going on, there seems to be "no visible
end to the struggle for recognition"[99] between actors that present themselves
as normative powers. It appears that, for the time being at least, normative
power Europe remains largely a continental phenomenon circumscribed by
the contours of EU-Europe and its neighborhood; normative power Japan
seems to be a niche phenomenon (in sectors such as human security and
climate change); while normative power China demonstrates a potential for a
contextual redefinition of the "normal" in different global locales. In the end,
however, one needs to acknowledge that the interpretation of any particular
enmeshment in global processes is subject to complex contingencies.[100]
Therefore, if it is to maintain its relevance, a normative power needs to
remain both attuned and committed to an ongoing practice of the definition
and redefinition of the normal in bilateral and multilateral contexts.

NOTES

1. There are many individuals whose contribution—both normative and otherwise—has influenced the shape of this research. I would like to acknowledge here the input of Jiun Bang, Yee-Kuang Heng, Ming-te Hung, Niv Horesh, Euikon Kim, Tony Tai-Ting Liu, Chengxin Pan, Yoneyuki Sugita, Tung-chieh Tsai, David Walton, Thomas Wilkins, and Brantly Womack, as well as the Mahmoud Pargoo for his superb research assistance. Also, the author wishes to thank the participants at the 2014 Asian Studies Congress (Torun, Poland), the 2014 annual meeting of the Academic Council of the UN System (Istanbul, Turkey), the 2014 International Symposium "Dynamics of the Asia-Pacific Region" at Osaka University (Japan) for their thoughtful and encouraging comments. Gratitude is also due to the Taiwanese National Science Council for providing a generous grant (#102EFA0501066) that facilitated this research and to the Graduate Institute for International Politics at the National Chung Hsing University (Tai-chung, Taiwan) for providing the most welcoming and stimulating hospitality. The usual caveat applies.

2. Kenneth W. Thompson, "The Study of International Politics: A Survey of Trends and Developments," *Review of Politics* 14, no. 4 (1952), pp. 433–67.

3. Torbjorn L. Knutsen, *History of International Relations Theory* (Manchester: Manchester University Press), p. 231.

4. Frederick H. Gareau, "The discipline International Relations: a multi-national perspective," *Journal of Politics* 43, no. 3 (1981), p. 779.

5. Stanley Hoffmann, "An American social science: international relations," *Daedalus* 106, no. 3 (1977), pp. 41–60.

6. Amitav Acharya and Barry Buzan, "Why is there no non-Western international relations theory? An introduction," *International Relations of the Asia-Pacific* 7, no. 3: 287–312.

7. Emilian Kavalski, *World Politics at the Edge of Chaos: Reflections on Complexity and Global Life* (Albany, NY: State University of New York Press, 2015).

8. Hans J. Morgenthau, "Vietnam: Shadow and substance," *New York Review of Books*, 16 (1965), p. 10.

9. Ian Manners, "Normative power Europe: a contradiction in terms?" *Journal of Common Market Studies* 40, no. 2 (2002), p. 253.

10. Jay Jackson, "Normative power and conflict potential," *Sociological Methods & Research* 4, no. 2 (1975), pp. 237–39.

11. Emilian Kavalski, "From the Western Balkans to the Greater Balkans Area: the external conditioning of 'awkward' and 'integrated' states." *Mediterranean Quarterly* 17, no. 3 (2006), pp. 86–100.

12. Joseph S. Nye, *Soft power: The means to success in world politics.* (New York: PublicAffairs, 2004), p. 5.

13. Linus Hagström and Bjorn Jerdén, "East Asia's power shift: The flaws and hazards of the debate and how to avoid them," *Asian Perspective* 38, no. 3 (2014), p. 347.

14. Ian Clark, "International Society and China: The Power of Norms and the Norms of Power," *Chinese Journal of International Politics* 7, np. 3 (2014), p. 320.

15. Peter Dauvergne and Déborah B.L. Farias, "The rise of Brazil as a global development power," *Third World Quarterly* 33, np. 5 (2012), pp. 903–17; Eleni Lazarou, "A model in crisis? Effects of the crisis in Europe on the influence of the EU as a model for regional integration in South America," Paper presented at the 2011 Annual Meeting of the International Studies Association Annual Conference, Montreal, QC

16. Emilian Kavalski, "Partnership or rivalry between the EU, China and India in Central Asia: The normative power of regional actors with global aspirations," *European Law Journal* 13, no. 6 (2007): 839–856; Emilian Kavalski, "Venus and the porcupine: Assessing the EU-India strategic partnership," South Asian Survey 15, no. 1 (2008), pp. 63–81; Emilian Kavalski, *Central Asia and the rise of normative powers: contextualizing the security governance of the European Union, China, and India* (New York: Bloomsbury, 2012); Emilian Kavalski, "'Pax Idica' or '"Brand India'? The Myth of Assertive Posturing in India's Post-1998 Foreign Policy-making," Harvard Asia Quarterly 14, no. 2 (2012), pp. 46–51; Emilian Kavalski, "The shadows of normative power in Asia: framing the international agency of China, India, and Japan,"

Pacific Focus 29, no. 3 (2014), pp. 303–28; Emilian Kavalski, 'The European Union and India: Birds of a Feather or Frenemies for Ever?' in Pascaline Winand, Andrea Benvenuti and M. Guderzo, eds, *The External Relations of the European Union* (New York: Peter Lang, 2015), pp. 151–66; Radha Kumar, "India as a Foreign Policy Actor–Normative Redux." In Nathali Tocci (Ed.), *Who is a normative foreign policy actor? The European Union and its Global Partners* (Brussels: Centre for European Policy Studies, 2008), pp. 211–64.

17. Emel Parlar Dal, "Assessing Turkey's Normative Power in the Middle East and North Africa Region: New Dynamics and their Limitations," *Turkish Studies* 14, no. 4 (2013), pp. 709–34.

18. Aleksey S. Makarychev, "Rebranding Russia: Norms, politics and power." In Nathali Tocci (Ed.), *Who is a Normative Foreign Policy Actor? The European Union and Its Global Partners* (Brussels: Centre for European Policy Studies), pp. 156–210; Jan Steinkohl, "Normative Power Rivalry? The European Union, Russia and the question of Kosovo," *College of Europe EU Diplomacy Paper,* no. 6 (2010).

19. Kei Koga, "The Normative Power of the 'ASEAN Way': Potentials, Limitations, and Implications for East Asian Regionalism," *Stanford Journal of East Asian Studies* 10, no. 1 (2010), pp. 80–95.

20. Van Jackson, "Power, trust, and network complexity: three logics of hedging in Asian security," *International Relations of the Asia-Pacific* 14, no. 3 (2014), p. 338.

21. Thomas Diez, "Constructing the Self and Changing Others: Reconsidering Normative Power Europe," *Millennium* 33, no. 3 (2005), p. 615.

22. Nathalie Tocci, "Proliferating normative foreign policy: The European Union and its global partners." In Nathalie Tocci (Ed.), *Who is a normative foreign policy actor? The European Union and its Global Partners.*(Brussels: Centre for European Policy Studies), pp. 1–23

23. Chengxin Pan, "Rethinking Chinese Power: A conceptual corrective to the 'power shift' narrative," *Asian Perspective* 38, no. 3 (2014), pp. 387–410.

24. Dirk Nabers, "Power, leadership, and hegemony in international politics: the case of East Asia," *Review of International Studies* 36, no. 4 (2010), pp. 931–49.

25. Jackson, "Normative power and conflict potential," pp. 237–63.

26. Pan, "Rethinking Chinese power," p. 403.

27. Edward H. Carr, *The twenty years' crisis, 1919–1939: an introduction to the study of international relations* (New York: Harper & Row), p. 236.

28. Nora Fisher Onar and Kalypso Nicolaïdis "The decentering agenda: Europe as a postcolonial power," *Cooperation & Conflict* 48, no.2 (2013), p. 285.

29. Xiaoyu Pu, "Socialization as a two-way process: Emerging powers and the diffusion of international norms," *Chinese Journal of International Politics* 5, no. 4 (2012), p. 365.

30. Kalevi J. Holsti, *Change in the international system: Essays on the theory and practice of international relations* (Aldershot: Edward Elgar, 1991), p. 19.

31. Emmanuel Adler, "The Spread of Security Communities: Communities of Practice, Self-Restraint, and NATO's Post-Cold War Transformation," *European Journal of International Relations* 14, no. 2 (2008), p. 203.

32. Pan, "Rethinking Chinese power," p. 393.

33. Steffano Guzzini, *Power, realism and constructivism* (New York: Routledge, 2014), p. 24.

34. Reinhard Wolf, "Respect and disrespect in international politics," *International Theory* 3, no. 1 (2011), p. 113. Emphasis in original.

35. Gary Goertz, *Contexts of International Politics* (Cambridge: Cambridge University Press, 1994).

36. Erik Ringmar, "Performing International Systems: Two East-Asian Alternatives to the Westphalian order." *International Organization* 66, no. 1 (2012), p. 19.

37. Mark Webber, *Inclusion, exclusion and the governance of European security* (Manchester: Manchester University Press, 2007).

38. Frank Schimmelfennig and Ulf Sedelmeier, *The Europeanization of central and eastern Europe.* (Ithaca, NY: Cornell University Press), p. 9.

39. Andrew Moravcsik, in Gustav Lindstrom, and Burkar Schmitt, eds, *Lessons from Iraq* (Paris: EU Institute for Security Studies, 2004), p. 191.

40. Ole Wæver, "European security identities," *JCMS: Journal of Common Market Studies* 34, no. 1 (1996), pp. 103–132.

41. Michael Smith, "Between 'soft power' and a hard place: European Union foreign and security policy between the Islamic world and the United States." *International Politics* 46, no. 5 (2009), p. 603.

42. Emilian Kavalski, *Extending the European Security Community* (London: I.B.Tauris, 2008).

43. Diez, "Constructing the Self and Changing Others," p. 614.

44. Onar and Nicolaïdis "The decentering agenda," p. 285.

45. Muthiah Alagappa, ed, *Asian Security Practice* (Stanford, CA: Stanford University Press, 1998).

46. Kavalski, "Partnership or Rivalry," pp. 839–56; Kavalski, *Central Asia and the Rise of Normative Powers*; Kavalski, "The Shadows of Normative Power," pp. 311–14; Emilian Kavalski, "Chinese Normative Communities of Practice," in Li Xing and Abdulkadir Osman Farah, eds, *China-Africa Relations in the Era of Great Transformations* (Farnham: Ashgate, 2013), 49–70; Emilian Kavalski, "The Struggle for Recognition of Normative Powers: Normative Power Europe and Normative Power China in Context," *Cooperation & Conflict* 48, no. 2 (2013), pp. 247–67; Emilian Kavalski, "Recognizing Chinese IR Theory" in Niv Horesh and Emilian Kavalski, eds, *Asian Thought on China's Changing International Relations* (London: Palgrave), pp. 230–48; Xiaoyu Pu, "Socialization as a two-way process;" Xiaoming Zhang, "A rising China and the normative changes in international society," *East Asia* 28, no. 3 (2010), pp. 235–46; Brantley Womack, "China as a normative foreign policy actor," in Natalie Tocci, ed, *Who is a normative foreign policy actor? The European Union and its global partners.* (Brussels: CEPS, 2008), pp. 265–300. Yi Wang, "The identity dilemmas of EU Normative Power: Observations from Chinese Traditional Culture," in André Gerrits, ed, *Normative power Europe in a changing world* (The Hague: Netherlands Institute of International Relations, 2009), pp. 67–76.

47. David P. Fidler, "Eastphalia Emerging? Asia, international law, and global governance," *Indiana Journal of International Law* 17, no. 1 (2010), pp. 1–12.

48. Geremie R. Barmé, *In the Red: On Contemporary Chinese Culture* (New York: Columbia University Press, 1999), p. 18.

49. Gloria Davis, *Worrying About China* (Cambridge, MA: Harvard University Press, 2007), p. 30.

50. Yee-Kuang Heng, "Mirror, mirror on the wall, who is the softest of them all? Evaluating Japanese and Chinese strategies in the 'soft' power competition era," *International Relations of the Asia-Pacific* 10, no. 2 (2010), pp. 275–304; Emilia Kavalski, "Shanghaied into cooperation: Framing China's socialization of Central Asia," *Journal of Asian and African Studies* 45, no. 2 (2010), pp. 131–45.

51. Davis, *Worrying About China*, p. 229.

52. Feng Zhang, "The Tsinghua approach and the inception of Chinese theories of international relations," *Chinese Journal of International Politics* 5, no. 1 (2012), p. 99.

53. Feng Zhang, "Regionalization in the Tianxia? Continuity and change in China's foreign policy," in Emilian Kavalski, ed, *China and the global politics of regionalization* (Farnham: Ashgate, 2009), p. 31.

54. Womack, "China as a normative foreign policy actor," pp. 294–97.

55. Tingyang Zhao, "Rethinking empire from the Chinese concept 'all-under-heaven'," *Social Identities* 12, no. 1 (2006), p. 35.

56. Henry Rosemont, "Two loci of authority: Autonomous individuals and related persons," in P.H. Hershock and R.T. Ames, eds, *Confucian cultures of authority* (Albany, NY: SUNY Press, 2006), p. 14.

57. Philip Nel, "Redistribution and recognition: What emerging regional powers want," *Review of International Studies* 36, no. 4 (2010), pp. 970–71.

58. Womack, "China as a normative foreign policy actor," pp. 295–97.

59. Yan Xuetong, *Ancient Chinese Thought, Modern Chinese Power* (Princeton, NJ: Princeton University Press, 2012), p. 238.

60. Emilian Kavalski, "'Do as I Do': The Global Politics of China's Regionalization" in Emilian Kavalski, ed, *China and the Global Politics of Regionalization* (Farnham: Ashgate, 2009), pp. 1–18. Emphasis in original.

61. *Time*, "Towards the Japanese Century," 2 March 1970, p. 39.

62. Isaac Shapiro, "The Risen Sun: Japanese Gaullism?" *Foreign Affairs* 41, no. 4 (1980/1981), p. 62.

63. Joseph S. Nye, "Coping with Japan," *Foreign Policy* 89, no. 1 (1992/1993), pp. 96–115; Joseph S. Nye, K.W. Dam, J.M. Deutch, and D. Rowe "Harnessing Japan: A U.S. Strategy for Managing Japan's Rise as a Global Power," *The Washington Quarterly* 16, no. 2 (1993), pp. 29–41.

64. Quoted in in Larry Martz, "The Hour of Power," *Newsweek* 9 (1989), p. 19.

65. *The Economist*, "Japan and America on a collision course," no. 7644 (1990), pp. 53–54.

66. George Friedman and Meredith LeBard, *The Coming War with Japan* (New York: St. Martin's Press, 1991).

67. Shapiro, "The Risen Sun," p. 62.

68. Sadako Ogata, "Japan's UN Policy in the 1980s," *Asian Survey* 27, no. 9 (1987), p. 965.

69. *Time*, "Towards the Japanese Century," p. 33.

70. Yee-Kuang Heng, "Beyond 'kawaii' pop culture: Japan's normative soft power as global trouble-shooter," *The Pacific Review* 24, no. 2 (2014), pp. 169–92; Kavalski, "The Shadows of Normative Power," pp. 318–21; Rok Zupančič and Miha Hribernik, "Normative Power Japan: The EU's ideational successor or another 'contradiction in terms'?" *Romanian Journal of Political Science* 13, no. 2 (2013), pp. 106–136; Rok Zupančič and Miha Hribernik, "'Discovering' Normative Power as a State Strategy in the framework of security, foreign, and defence policy: The Case of Japan," *Philippine Political Science Journal* 35, no. 1 (2014), pp. 78–97.

71. Ezra F. Vogel, "Pax Nipponica?" *Foreign Affairs* 64, no. 4 (1986), pp. 752–67.

72. Kent Calder quoted in Martz, "The Hour of Power," p. 15.

73. Marvin Soroos, "Global Interdependence and the Responsibilities of States: Learning from the Japanese Experience," *Journal of Peace Research* 25, no. 1 (1988), p. 28.

74. Richard Stubbs, "Reluctant Leader, Expectant Followers: Japan and Southeast Asia," *International Journal* 46, no. 4, (1991), p. 667.

75. Nobuo Okawara and Peter J. Katzenstein, "Japan and Asian-Pacific Security: regionalization, entrenched bilateralism, and incipient multilateralism," in Peter J. Katzenstein, ed, *Rethinking Japanese Security: Internal and external dimensions*, London: Routledge: 2008), pp. 104–132.

76. Rok Zupančič and Miha Hribernik, "Normative Power Japan," pp. 106–136.

77. Heng, "Mirror, Mirror on the Wall," pp. 275–304; Hsien-Li Tan, "Not just global rhetoric: Japan's substantive actualization of its human security foreign policy," *International Relations of the Asia-Pacific* 10, no. 1 (2010), pp. 159–87.

78. Heng, "Beyond 'Kawaii' Pop Culture," pp. 169–92.

79. Michael J. Green, "Japan Is Back: Why Tokyo's new assertiveness is good for Washington," *Foreign Affairs* 86, no. 2 (2007), p. 144.

80. Heng, "Beyond 'Kawaii' Pop Culture," p. 191.

81. Zupančič and Hribernik, "Normative Power Japan," pp. 106–136.

82. Heng, "Beyond 'Kawaii' Pop Culture," pp. 169–92.

83. Stubbs, "Reluctant leader, expectant followers," pp. 649–67; Heng, "Mirror, Mirror on the Wall," pp. 275–304.

84. Emilian Kavalski, "The Struggle for Recognition of Normative Powers: Normative Power Europe and Normative Power China in Context," *Cooperation & Conflict* 48, no. 2 (2013), pp. 247–67.

85. Florian Schneider, "Reconceptualizing World Order: Chinese Political Thought and Its Challenge to International Relations Theory," *Review of International Studies* 40, no. 4 (2014), p. 702.

86. Nel, "Redistribution and recognition," p. 102.

87. Stubbs, "Reluctant leader, expectant followers," p. 652.

88. Webber, *Inclusion, exclusion and the governance of European security*, 4.

89. Axel Honneth, "Recognition between States," in T. Lindermann and Erik Ringmar, eds, *The International Politics of Recognition* (Boulder, CO: Paradigm), p. 34

90. Paul H. Appleby, "Managing Complexity," *Ethics* 64, no. 2 (1954), p. 96.

91. Patchen Markell, *Bound by Recognition* (Princeton, NJ: Princeton University Press, 2003), p. 36.

92. Stubbs, "Reluctant leader, expectant followers," p. 653.

93. Emilian Kavalski, "The Fifth Debate and the Emergence of Complex International Relations Theory," *Cambridge Review of International Affairs* 20, no. 3 (2007), pp. 435–54.

94. Headley Bull, *The Anarchical Society: A Study of Order in World Politics* (Basingstoke: Macmillan, 1977), p. 96. Emphasis added.

95. Morgenthau, "Vietnam: Shadow and substance," p. 10.

96. Clark, "International Society and China," p. 337.

97. Womack, "China as a normative foreign policy actor," p. 226.

98. Wæver, "European security identities," p. 127.

99. Jürgen Haacke, "The Frankfurt School and International Relations: On the Centrality of Recognition," *Review of International Studies* 31, no. 1 (2005), p. 188.

100. Emilian Kavalski, "The International Politics of Fusion and Fissure in the Awkward States of Post-Soviet Central Asia," in Emilian Kavalski, ed, *Stable Outside, Fragile Inside? Post-Soviet Statehood in Central Asia* (Aldershot: Ashgate), pp. 3–33.

Chapter Seven

The Asia-Europe Meeting (ASEM)

A Role for the European Union in Asia?

Bart Gaens, Senior Research Fellow,
the Finnish Institute of International Affairs

It has become commonplace to refer to the shift of economic power from West to East and from the Atlantic to the Pacific, and to highlight the regained prominence of Asia in global economy as well as politics. The world is now decidedly more multipolar and actors such as Russia, China or India are challenging the economic hegemony of the US and the European Union (EU). At the same time emerging powers in Asia are increasingly eager to counterbalance the global influence of the West. The EU on the other hand is still in the process of recovering from the Eurozone crisis, but at the same time the debate continues on a much-needed larger global role for Europe, not only as an economic power, but also as a political and security actor including in Asia.

Following the US rebalancing to the Asia-Pacific, some observers have even referred to the EU's very own "pivot to Asia", which started around a decade ago.[1] It cannot be denied that the EU, as an entity still the world's largest economy, has strongly vested interests in Asia and that overarching EU-Asia relations have grown considerably. In 2012 Asian countries accounted for 29.8% of EU imports and 21.4% of exports, and between 2008 and 2012 trade grew annually on average by 5.8%.[2] Four Asian countries (China, Japan, India and South Korea) are among the EU's top ten trading partners. The EU has also established free-trade agreements (FTAs) with South Korea and Singapore, an FTA with Vietnam is nearing completion, and negotiations are continuing with Japan, Malaysia, India, and Thailand. Taken together, Asia and Europe (defined as the current members of the

Asia-Europe Meeting or ASEM) carry considerable weight. The population of ASEM countries represents 62.5% of the world population.[3] In 2012 57% of the global GDP was created in ASEM countries, with Europe accounting for almost a quarter and the Asian grouping producing almost a third of the total.[4] 26% of EU outward investment goes to Asia with a particular focus on China and Australia, India, Indonesia and Korea. Inward investment in the EU is growing, and China, Korea and Thailand were the most important investors in 2012. Exports from the EU to Asian ASEM countries rose sharply in 2012 for a total of 562 billion euro, while imports amounted to 809 billion.[5]

As a political player however, the EU is much less visible in the region. The EU has certainly increased its political actorness since the 1990s, now displaying greater continuity and visibility, and possessing more capability to speak with one voice through its "foreign ministry", the European External Action Service (EEAS) and stronger links between Commission, Council and High Representative for Foreign Affairs and Security Policy. But contrary to the optimism of early 1990s of being able to play a greater global role, the EU seems to have lost some of its missionary zeal as a normative power, and is now much less confident that its own successful integration model can be copied by other regions in the world. In Asia in particular the EU as a political actor is relatively absent. Geographical distance certainly plays a role, but also the colonial past, the EU's lack of military power, and human rights concerns can be cited as causal factors.

In security terms the EU's presence in Asia is limited. The EU has been a member of the ASEAN Regional Forum (ARF) since 1994 and of ASEM since 1996. In 2012 the EU acceded to the Treaty of Amity and Cooperation in Southeast Asia (TAC), a condition for a prospective future participation in the East Asia Summit (EAS). Significantly, the EU has assisted democratic transitions in East Timor and Cambodia, mediated in peace negotiations in Aceh, Indonesia, and was involved in conflict resolution in the Philippines, with a greater forthcoming role in civilian capacity building initiatives in Myanmar.[6] Five of the EU's most important "strategic partners" are located in the broadly defined Asian region (China, India, Japan, Korea and Russia). Europe does not have a military presence in Asia, but plays an (often neglected) important role as an arms exporter, sometimes at a par with the US, accompanied by cooperation, training, services and upgrades.[7]

Given the fact that the EU, unlike the US, does not have any formal military alliances in the region, Europe has tended to focus on the promotion of multilateralism. However, in a changing global environment and faced with internal crises, the notion that the EU still "punches below its weight politically" has led to continued calls for a new global strategy in order to achieve greater global political presence. The EU has multiple tools to its disposal to accomplish that aim, including bilateral, interregional, and multilateral relations. It is the aim of this chapter to shed light on one of the most important fora that combines these three forms of interaction and constitutes the prime nodal point of relations between countries of both regions, namely the Asia-Europe Meeting (ASEM). Bilateral links between the European Community (EC) and ASEAN arose already in 1978 with the first ASEAN-EC ministerial conference. However, it was only after the publication of the European Union's New Asia Strategy of 1994 and the ensuing start of the Asia-Europe Meeting (ASEM) in 1996 that interregional relations between a gradually integrating yet diffuse East Asian region and the EU took off. Conceived in the post-Cold War environment of the early 1990s, ASEM reflected the European objective of taking part in the swiftly growing East Asian economies, but more importantly it expressed EU ambitions to play a greater global political role.

Focusing on the role of the EU, the following analysis explores ASEM as an international institution with idiosyncratic features that nevertheless are in a constant process of adaptation to a changing world. As such, fora such as ASEM are important markers reflecting changes in global governance, shifting power balances, advances in regional integration, and transforming alliances. Concretely this chapter examines the features and changing contours of ASEM as an international institution, aiming to answer four questions: first, what are the features of ASEM's institutional design in terms of membership, scope, centralization, control and flexibility, and how do they tie in with the forum's objectives? Second, how do global changes in the importance that states attach to multilateralism, regionalism and bilateralism affect ASEM? Third, what are the normative considerations and the collective values underlying the sources of the preferences at the core of the institution, and can a process towards convergence in norms and values between Europe and Asia be detected? And fourth, what role can ASEM play as a platform promoting security cooperation between Asia and Europe, and more specifically, how can it promote the EU's involvement in Asia as an actor in the field of soft security?

ASEM'S INSTITUTIONAL DESIGN

International institutions reveal a wide diversity in set-up, goals, organization, working methods and approach. While some are heavily codified and formal, others are much looser and informal, to the point of barely being visible. They can therefore be defined in the broadest possible terms as "relatively stable sets of related constitutive, regulative, and procedural norms and rules that pertain to the international system, the actors in the system (including states as well as nonstate entities), and their activities".[8] This brings to the fore the question of how European and Asian states design institutions to facilitate so-called interregional relations. As argued by the "Rational Design of International Institutions" (RDII) research project, "states use international institutions to further their own goals, and they design institutions accordingly".[9] Looking at ASEM's stated goals, as a "club of like-minded partners" it was not intended to be a forum for negotiating agreements, but rather to function as a political catalyst, to promote common interests in global fora and to identify priorities for concerted action in pursuit of these common interests. The prime goal was to achieve "mutual understanding and enhanced awareness through dialogue".[10]

With these objectives in mind, how was ASEM as an institution designed? Koremenos et al. [11] have proposed five key dimensions that determine variation among the plethora of international institutions:

- Membership rules (MEMBERSHIP): Is membership exclusive and restrictive, or inclusive; is it regional or global; and is it restricted to states or are other actors involved?
- Scope of issues covered (SCOPE): is the scope limited or comprehensive, and are the issues dealt with interlinked or not?
- Centralization of tasks (CENTRALIZATION): are institutional tasks performed by a single focal entity (i.e. does the institution display actorness) and to what extent are the different activities centralized?
- Rules for controlling the institution (CONTROL): how are collective decisions made, do all members carry equal weight, and can a minority hold veto power?
- Flexibility of arrangements (FLEXIBILITY): how do institutional rules and procedures accommodate new circumstances and challenges?

Based on these five key dimensions, the following section will provide an overview of how ASEM as the prime Asia-Europe interregional institution is designed.

Membership

ASEM membership is open, evolutionary, inclusive and conducted on the basis of consensus. The first ASEM summit took place in 1996 with 26 participants, 15 EU member states plus the European Commission, and seven-member ASEAN (Association of Southeast Asian Nations) in addition to China, Japan and the Republic of Korea. Now, nearly twenty years later, the forum has evolved dramatically in terms of membership, after having gone through several stages of enlargement. Ten new EU member states joined in 2004, while the Asian group enlarged to include Cambodia, Laos and Burma/Myanmar. India, Pakistan, Mongolia and the ASEAN Secretariat entered the partnership in 2006, after the EU had further come to include

Romania and Bulgaria. The total reached 48 after Russia, Australia and New Zealand joined the gathering in 2010. Bangladesh and non-EU states Switzerland and Norway were allowed to join in 2012. In October 2014 Croatia formally joined, while ASEM expanded into Central Asia with the membership of Kazakhstan, to make a total of 53 partners.

Scope

The scope of issues dealt with in ASEM are highly comprehensive. The stated objective is to carry forward three key dimensions or pillars: fostering political dialogue, reinforcing economic cooperation, and promoting cooperation in other areas (cultural, social, and people-to-people). Issues have become increasingly interlinked. Connectivity, for example, an issue featuring prominently in the tenth summit in Milan in October 2014, relates to economic integration, trade and investment but also has ramifications for sustainable development, think tank and research or educational communities, and political linkages.

Centralization

ASEM lacks a secretariat, and as an informal process is only very loosely institutionalized. It does include one institution, the Asia-Europe Foundation (ASEF) which focuses on the third pillar (cooperation in the socio-cultural dimension). From the organizational perspective ASEM follows an interregional group-to-group structure, making a clear distinction between a European and an Asian grouping (as is obvious in the frequent references to the term "mutual"). On the other hand the membership asymmetry, the dialogue arrangements and the interaction with business communities as well as civil society point justify labeling ASEM a transregional forum. Management of the process takes place at the sub-regional level, in the case of the EU through the European External Action Service. At the same time ASEM contains a strong intergovernmental dimension, visible in the projects run under the ASEM umbrella and headed by "shepherd groups" of individual states from Europe and Asia. Bilateral contacts between government leaders furthermore constitute an important element of the biennial summits. Lastly, ASEM also provides a framework for bilateral contacts in the sidelines of the summit taking place between the EU and single powers.

Control

ASEM aimed to "foster a relation between equals in the spirit of partnership", hence excluding issues such as development aid. EU member states sought to re-establish ties with former in Southeast Asia, while at the same time engaging or increasing interaction with other countries, including in

Northeast Asia. The emphasis therefore has always been on equality and consensus. No negotiations or decisions take place, but coordination takes place on a regional basis. To decide on membership enlargement for example, a candidate country first needs to get support among the partners of its own region, before acquiring the approve of all the participants in the other region.

Flexibility

ASEM as an informal and loosely institutionalized structure is highly flexible. As argued by Lipson[12] , informality is a device to minimize the impediments to cooperation. It offers advantages of flexibility, speed, privacy and simplicity. Informal agreements or structures allow for easy adaptation to changed circumstances, and for a speedier process of conclusion. It also makes agreements less constraining than diplomatic precedents, and at the same time offers a lower profile: close scrutiny by the general public or agencies with different agendas can be avoided. ASEM is a seemingly very Asian structure, closely incorporating elements of the so-called ASEAN Way and involving a high degree of discretion, privacy, pragmatism, informality, consensus-building, non-confrontation and non-interference. This is often contrasted with "Western" regional and multilateral institutions that rely much more on formal organization and legalistic decision-making procedures.[13]

So how does this "Asian" institutional design fit the EU's stated goal to increase its political presence in Asia? As argued by Alexander Wendt, the "rational" choice for a certain institutional structure is subjective, in that it aims to help the actors involved how to solve a perceived collective-action problem.[14] From the European perspective, the "logic of appropriateness" played an important role: the institutional design was chosen not by weighing costs and benefits, but on the basis of what is normatively appropriate. In other words, in order to attribute to a rising Asia in the mid-1990s a status more appropriate to its increasing global weight, and to enable the discussion of sensitive or contentious issues on the basis of equality, the EU followed the ASEAN Way, as promoted strongly by Singapore, one of ASEM's initial driving forces.

As furthermore posited by Wendt, as a next step we need to examine institutional effectiveness.[15] Have expectations missed the mark, or did the design features have unintended negative consequences? Have institutional choices been subjectively rational, but objectively a mistake? In terms of membership, ASEM's inclusive and approach has turned it into an unwieldy, diffuse and even "bloated" gathering of 53 members. The forum has therefore not inaccurately been criticized as a talking shop without tangible objectives. In terms of its comprehensive scope, the forum is said to have been unable to play any significant role in contributing to global governance. As a vehicle for "soft politics"[16] that can only make an indirect contribution to other global institutions, ASEM's impact has been minimal, and examples of thereof are few.

ASEM's lack of centralization, loose control and non-institutionalization stand in contrast to the occasionally lofty expectations held by participants. For example, the stated goal by EU member states such as France of "completing the third leg of the triangle", in other words trying to match the strongly developed Transatlantic ties and the vital link between the US and Asia, was doomed from the beginning. ASEM never possessed the instruments to help balance the influence of the US in military and security terms in the Asian region. Furthermore, from the outset it has been clear that participants were unwilling to endanger relations with US, or were simply too divided to take meaningful collective action against US interests.[17] Today, in view of the ongoing Transatlantic Trade and Investment Partnership (TTIP) free trade negotiations and the events in the Crimea, transatlantic solidarity has increased and has led to a re-confirmation of "the West" and "Western values", resulting in an even stronger view of the US as the key security provider in Asia. In addition to the discrepancy between institutional design and expectations, different emphases by partner countries have resulted in a plethora of initiatives and projects, sometimes without focus or connection to the summit-level dialogue.

In spite of these "failures" in terms of institutional effectiveness, however, ASEM has achieved success in three fields, all owing to the forum's flexibility. First, it has effectively adapted to global changes and to the shifting importance that states attach to multilateralism, regionalism and bilateralism. Second, its informal approach and emphasis on dialogue has resulted in the formation of a certain collective identity, and arguably even in a gradual process of convergence in norms and values. Third, ASEM is increasingly shaping itself as an appropriate platform for dialogue as well as cooperation between Europe and Asia on issues relating to non-traditional security. These three accomplishments will be discussed in the sections below.

ADAPTATION TO GLOBAL CHANGES

As argued by Koremenos et al., institutions are rational, negotiated responses to the problems international actors face.[18] As such they are "incentive capable", created and adapted according to the interests of the actors involved, and also shaping other institutions. ASEM's process of adaptation clearly reflects a rapid process of adjustment to a perceived failure of (or at least a lesser role attributed to) multilateralism in global governance, and to a diminished role given to interregionalism to the expense of bilateralism.

First, ASEM's role in what has come to be known as "patchwork govern-ance" has increased. Patchwork governance is a term that has been used in the context of climate change negotiations. In other words, when negotiations under the UN or WTO umbrella stall, as a second best option "a broad coalition of ambitious and pragmatic countries, regions, cities, companies, media, non-governmental organizations, and thought leaders contributes to the emergence of a complex, multilayered governance landscape".[19] In re-cent years ASEM is increasingly focusing on "variable geometry" or the idea that different interests and priorities should allow for the shaping informal functional groups of states that drive forward tangible cooperation through "coalitions". The concept of such an "issue-based leadership" as guiding tool was first launched at the Helsinki ASEM6 summit, but its implementation was flawed, suffering from relatively low commitment, little information-sharing and follow-up. The idea was however revived in 2013, and currently twelve areas for cooperation run by different groups of states have been outlined, including on sustainable water management, energy efficiency technology, vocational training, food safety and small-and-medium-sized companies (SME) cooperation. In this sense ASEM can be regarded as one forum available for "forum shopping". Jürgen Rüland has argued that the "principled multilateralism" of the immediate post-Cold War period is in crisis and gradually giving way to "diminished multilateralism". As a result, when states feel that multilateral fora are not yielding results, they establish new ones or pick and choose among those that best suit their individual political agendas.[20] Through its variable geometry, ASEM can cater to the individual political agendas of member states, in order to complement coop-eration in other fora.

At least as importantly however, ASEM serves as a signpost of the "changing interlinkages of bilateral, regional and transregional relations that the EU has around the globe".[21] Interregionalism, championed by the EU, has been hailed as a new layer in the system of global governance. Currently however, its importance has dwindled. Rather than pursuing pure region-to-region relations with East Asia, as formerly was the case, the EU at present aims to establish differentiated interregional relationships with a much stronger role given to bilateral and transregional relations, in other words pursue "complex interregionalism".[22] In my view, ASEM can be regarded as a suitable example. While retaining the interregional setup, bilateral contacts in ASEM have only increased in importance. In the margins of ASEM sum-mits, a multitude of bilateral meetings take place. These offer economies of scale, allowing states to gain time and expenses by setting up a number of bilateral meetings in the sidelines of summits. At the same time they allow for small states to meet with bigger ones, bridging the gap to the G20 for example, and they allow for meeting with states that are normally not on the radar, or that are officially seen as "problematic partners".

COMMUNICATIVE RATIONALITY AND NORMATIVE CONVERGENCE

In addition to its flexibility enabling smooth adaptation to global shifts, ASEM's focus on informality and loose institutionalization has also resulted in an affirmation of the importance of dialogue and communication, and arguably even in a slowly-developing convergence in norms and values. As an informal dialogue process ASEM is in the first place about communication. The forum allows for an informal exchange of views, experiences, and expertise on any topical and relevant political issue. It is beyond doubt that ASEM can function as a valuable tool to foster closer personal and professional relationships between leaders of states and representatives of regions, promoting dialogue and habits of cooperation. It is therefore "a high-level dialogue, not an institution, not a "regional United Nations" where leaders need to go on record on political issues or other issues in reading out well prepared statements, without engaging with others. Dialogue in itself is a goal contributing to the unique character of the ASEM process".[23] To phrase it in Habermasian terms, for the EU ASEM is rooted in communicative rationality, rather than strategic or instrumental rationality. Whereas the former approach places Self and Other as members of the same community and is aimed at achieving consensus or understanding, the latter approach is driven by power and interest and posits a Self opposite an Other.[24]

This observation is interesting because of the standard view of "Western" states placing emphasis on achievement and legalization, in contrast to Asian states seeing dialogue as an accomplishment in itself. This stereotypical perspective has been confirmed by the European Commission itself: "While Asian partners regard dialogue in itself as an achievement and prefer to talk about non-contentious issues, Europeans tend to press for tangible results and are interested to take up contentious issues in order to arrive at conclusions".[25] Nevertheless, at present it is rather the Asian states in ASEM that are pressuring the European side for the achievement of more concrete outcomes. The strongest promoter of the above-mentioned issue-based leadership for example was India. The European side on the other hand seems to prefer to maintain ASEM as a "talking shop".[26] ASEM's lack of a clear, relevant role in global governance, due to the open and non-binding approach, has led to repeated calls for institutionalization, in the first place through the establishment of an ASEM secretariat in order to enhance achievement orientation. The EU however is opposed to institutionalization and the creation of a secretariat. For the EU, ASEM is perhaps limited in legalistic terms, but at the same time it offers a highly adaptable, multidimensional and all-encompassing framework for interaction. Policy issues can be dealt with at the summits, in the different ministerial meetings, or at the track-two level, and can easily be moved up and down a hierarchy depending on their importance and sensitivity which makes ASEM "an expandable box of opportunities".[27]

Many more reasons can be found. Institutionalization would generate matters related to staffing, funding and location, and could even slow down the process as it potentially conflicts with the existing EU coordination machinery. In addition, cooperation with Asia could jeopardize the EU's privileged relation with North America. In addition, it would place ASEM closer to other, more formal international organizations, thereby losing its "added-value". Furthermore, the EU's emphasis on informality may not be surprising. First of all, Europe itself is not a unitary actor and is also divided, and we only have to think about the issue of Turkey's membership to the EU, but also the Turkish application to join ASEM, that reveals very strong dividing lines within Europe. Informality can thus be a way to more easily keep all member states happy, and it could offer the best way to integrate the mixed interests of the different intra-EU levels.

In sum, the view that Europeans necessarily pursue formal and legalized structures needs to be refuted. In addition, as Kahler has shown for the case of the Asia-Pacific region, also in Asian institutions choices for or against legalization are not grounded in pre-set cultural dispositions, but in "hard calculations of institutional performance and regional outcomes."[28] Institutions are a means to an end, and the choice for their design is strategic.

Finally, can we speak of an ASEM collective identity and has there been a convergence of values and norms? As argued by Wendt, "over time designs cause designers as much as designers cause designs".[29] In other words, initial institutional design play a feedback role and have an impact on the actors who join the institution at a later stage. Furthermore, institutional design has an effect on identities and interests, resulting in a collective identity, valuing the institution as an end in itself rather than a means to an end. Once foundational normative principles are fixed, subsequent institutional developments will follow from the implications of that normative logic.[30]

As such it can be argued that the initial approach of "constructive engagement" is still at the core of the forum, and shared by both regions. Compromise and "agreeing to disagree" is a vital component of communication when issues under discussion conflict with interests and identities.[31] In ASEM's early years, the EU has utilized the forum to show its emphasis on dialogue rather than confrontation and sanctions, by adopting an initially German-French strategy of problem-solving behind closed doors.[32] The EU has furthermore pursued a policy of "strategic adaptation" in order to adjust to Asian interests.[33] Given the legacy of Europe-Asia relations, any other approach may have obstructed progress entirely. It has allowed the EU to make use of ASEM as a political forum to address so-called sensitive issues while avoiding taking the moral high ground. After 1998 the emphasis on human rights through informal dialogue has steadily increased, primarily through ASEF-organised seminars, with Sweden and France as the main proponents. At the very least, the seminars have led to "an understanding of human rights similar to a minimum principled consensus".[34] This consensus-building process may indicate the way forward in the light of the EU's weakened profile as a normative power.

ASEM AS A FORUM TACKLING NON-TRADITIONAL SECURITY

Since the beginning of the 2000s the awareness has grown that, as a result of globalization, the global security agenda is increasingly determined by "new", "soft" or "non-traditional" security challenges, such as migrations, transnational crime, illicit trafficking, environmental degradation, disaster management, infectious diseases, etc. Especially since 9/11 new and "non-traditional" security challenges have appeared on the agenda. As defined by Collins, "(i)t is the centrality of the use, or threat to use, military force for coercive purposes that distinguishes traditional security from non-traditional security (NTS)."[35] In addition, the principal concern is not so much to safeguard territorial sovereignty, but society, communities, and people. As direct state-to-state military threats have declined in relative importance, soft, non-military security has become more salient, resulting in an increased importance of conflict prevention/management/avoidance, rather than combat operations.[36]

As a result ASEM has increasingly been focusing on this field of NTS, even if it has remained mainly at the level of consensus-building and informal consultations in the form of meetings aiming to share experiences and build a common agenda. As a multilateral, open and informal institution ASEM is ideally placed to tackle NTS, because it does not lock partners into rigid governmental positions.[37] At least the following initiatives have been launched:

- ASEM Anti-Money Laundering Initiative
- ASEM Initiative on Trafficking in Women and Children
- ASEM Ministerial Conference on Cooperation for the Management of Migratory Flows
- ASEM Symposium on Law Enforcement Organs' Cooperation in Combating Transnational Crime
- ASEM Anti-Corruption Initiative
- ASEM Cooperation in Promoting Awareness in the Young Generation on the Drug Problem

In recent years numerous projects have been added, from water management and climate change to maritime security and disaster vulnerability.

Furthermore, joint international customs operations have achieved tangible outcomes. In 2007, 2009 and 2014 Member States of ASEM and the European Anti-Fraud Office (OLAF) collaborated with Interpol, Europol and the World Customs Organization (WCO) in large-scale operations to counter smuggling of excise goods such as tobacco and alcohol. The success of these operations clearly shows that informal dialogue can be complemented by cooperation on the ground in tackling issues such as transnational organized crime.

CONCLUSION

The EU has long-standing ambitions to play a larger global role including in Asia, not only as an economic power but also as a political and security actor. This has only exacerbated since the self-declared rebalancing towards Asia by the US. Given the fact that the EU cannot play a hard military role, it has tended to focus on the promotion of multilateralism in the Asian region. The Asia-Europe Meeting or ASEM has been a prime tool to accomplish that aim through an interregional approach. The institutional design chosen to further the EU's objectives was "Asian-style" in origin, with a focus on inclusiveness, comprehensiveness, dialogue, consensus, equality and non-institutionalization. The EU may have chosen this approach out of the "logic of appropriateness", in consideration of a perceived set of norms and values held by its Asian counterpart.

When evaluating ASEM's effectiveness, it cannot be denied that the forum's design has not achieved great results. ASEM has enlarged to the point of being unwieldy, and it has remained at the level of a talking shop without substantial impact on other fora for global governance. Importantly the informal approach has often formed a mismatch with lofty proclaimed objectives. As such, ASEM has not contributed much to place the EU more firmly on the map as a political actor in Asia.

The institution's design, in particular its flexibility, however, did result in three important outcomes. First, ASEM has smoothly adapted to important changes in the global environment, including increased multipolarity and a transforming and convoluted interregionalism. This gives it more chances to play a meaningful role in the context of "patchwork governance", "diminished multilateralism", and "forum shopping". Second, ASEM's emphasis on "communicative rationality" confirms the perpetual need for dialogue. The process, which will celebrate its twentieth anniversary in 2016, may have even contributed to the gradual development of a collective identity and a convergence in norms and values, contributing to the EU's (strategic) acceptance of informal dialogue as a value. In a sense the EU has become more Asian than the Asians. Importantly, the EU has succeeded in establishing a forum for "constructive engagement" and political dialogue to complement its economic agenda, arguably even leading to a slow consensus-building process on sensitive issues such as human rights and the participation of civil society. Last but not least, ASEM has gradually been focusing more on non-traditional security. Progress made in the area of NTS is proof that Europe can play a "soft" role in Asian security, while at the same time pointing out the way forward for ASEM as an institution. It seems beyond doubt that the importance of ASEM's political and security-related dialogue and cooperation will only increase further alongside Asia's growing economic weight.

NOTES

1. Nicola Casarini, "The European Pivot," *Alert Asia* 3, EUISS (2013).
2. European External Action Service, "EU-Asia Factsheet 2014," *EEAS*, 14 July 2014, http://eeas.europa.eu/asia/docs/eu_in_asia_factsheet_en.pdf.
3. Eurostat, "ASEM and EU – Key Statistical Indicators," *Eurostat*, April 2014, http://ec.europa.eu/eurostat/statistics-explained/index.php/Asia-Europe_Meeting_(ASEM)_and_EU_-_key_statistical_indicators.
4. Ibid.
5. Ibid.
6. Casarini, "The European Pivot."
7. François Godement, "Divided Asia. The Implications for Europe," *European Council on Foreign Relations Policy Brief*, 22 November (2013).
8. John Duffield, "What are International Institutions?" *International Studies Review* 9 (2007), p. 8.
9. Barbara Koremenos, Charles Lipson and Duncan Snidal, "The Rational Design of International Institutions," *International Organization* 55, no. 4 (2001), p. 762.
10. European Commission, "Perspectives and Priorities for the ASEM Process," *European Commission*, SEC(97)1239 final. 26 June (1997), http://eeas.europa.eu/asem/docs/comm_working_doc_perspectives_priorities_asem_en.pdf.
11. Koremenos et al. "The Rational Design of International Institutions," p. 763.
12. Charles Lipson, "Why Are Some International Agreements Informal?" *International Organization* 45, no. 4 (1991), p. 500.
13. Jochen Prantl, "Multilateralism in East Asia: The Good, the Bad, and the Ugly," *TheAsanForum,* 23 May (2014). http://www.theasanforum.org/multilateralism-in-east-asia-the-good-the-bad-and-the-ugly/.
14. Alexander Wendt, "Driving with the Rearview Mirror. On the Rational Science of Institutional Design," *International Organization*, 55, no. 4 (2001), p. 1043.
15. Ibid.
16. Hanns W. Maull and Nuria Ofken, "Comparing Interregionalism. The Asia-Pacific Economic Cooperation (APEC) and the Asia-Europe Meeting (ASEM)," in *Interregionalism and International Relations*, ed. Heiner Hänggi, Ralf Roloff and Jürgen Rüland (London: Routledge, 2006).
17. Davis B. Bobrow, "The US and ASEM: Why the Hegemon Didn't Bark," *Pacific Review* 12, no. 1 (1999), p. 5.
18. Koremenos et al. "The Rational Design of International Institutions," 768.
19. Hale, Thomas et al., "Beyond a Global Deal: a UN+ Approach to Climate Governance," *Global Governance 2020*, 7 February (2011). http://www.globalpolicyjournal.com/articles/climate-change-energy-and-sustainability/beyond-global-deal-un-approach-climate-governance.
20. Jürgen Rüland, "The Rise of 'Diminished Multilateralism': East Asian and European Forum Shopping in Global Governance," *Asia Europe Journal* 9, no. 2-4 (2012).

21. Francis Baert, Tiziana Scaramagli, and Fredrik Söderbaum, "Introduction: Intersecting Interregionalism," in *Intersecting Interregionalism. Regions, Global Governance and the EU*, ed. Francis Baert, Tiziana Scaramagli, and Fredrik Söderbaum, Dordrecht: Springer (2014), p. 9.

22. Alan Hardacre and Michael Smith, "The European Union and the Contradictions of Complex Interregionalism," in *Intersecting Interregionalism*, ed. Baert et al., pp. 92-95.

23. European Commission, "Vademecum: Modalities for Future ASEM Dialogue – Taking the Process Forward," *Directorate General for External Relations*, 18 July (2001), p. 2. http:// www.aseminfoboard.org/sites/default/files/documents/vade.pdf.

24. See Wendt, "Driving with the Rearview Mirror," p. 1046.

25. European Commission, "Vademecum", p. 2.

26. David Fouquet, "Preparations for Milan ASEM Summit launched amid uncertainty," *Asian News Outlook*, European Institute for Asian Studies, 5 May (2014). http://www.eias.org/ asian-news-outlook/preparations-milan-asem-summit-launched-amid-uncertainty.

27. Anthony Forster, "The European Union in South-East Asia: Continuity and Change in Turbulent Times," *International Affairs* 75, no. 4 (1999), p. 753.

28. Miles Kahler, "Legalization as Strategy: The Asia-Pacific Case," *International Organization* 54, no. 3 (2000), p. 571.

29. Wendt, "Driving with the Rearview Mirror," p. 1033.

30. Ibid., p. 1039.

31. Maria-Gabriela Manea, "Human Rights and the Interregional Dialogue Between Asia and Europe: ASEAN-EU Relations and ASEM," *Pacific Review* 21, no. 3 (2008), p. 381.

32. See Bart Gaens, "The Development of the EU's Asia Strategy with Special Reference to China and India: Driving Forces and New Directions," in *The Role of the European Union in Asia: China and India as Strategic Partners*, ed. Bart Gaens, Juha Jokela and Eija Limnell, Farnham: Ashgate (2009), p. 69.

33. Manea, "Human Rights and the Interregional Dialogue Between Asia and Europe", pp. 380-81.

34. Ibid., p. 383.

35. Alan Collins, "Non-traditional security," in *Routledge Handbook of Asian Regionalism*, eds. Mark Beeson and Richard Stubbs, London: Routledge (2012), p. 314.

36. Roberto Menotti, Ferrucio Pastore and Manuel Rosini. "The new security agenda." In *Strengthening International Order*. Council for Asia-Europe Cooperation (CAEC), CAEC Task Force Reports. Tokyo and London: Council for Asia-Europe Cooperation (2000), pp. 160-61.

37. Ibid., p. 172.

Index

Acquisition and Cross-Servicing
Agreement (ACSA), 95
ACSA. *See* Acquisition and Cross-
Servicing Agreement
Action Plan, 94
ADIZ. *See* Air Defence Identification Zone
AFNC. *See* Air Force Nurse Corps
African Americans, 35
Agreed Framework (Geneva Agreement),
17–18
AIIB. *See* Asian Infrastructure Investment
Bank
Air Defence Identification Zone (ADIZ),
76, 83, 88
Air Force Nurse Corps (AFNC), 28, 29, 36,
37, 43, 46, 47
Air Identification Air Defence Zone, 99
anarchy, 6, 120
Arab-Israeli dispute, 67
ASEAN Regional Forum (ARF), 128
ASEF. *See* Asia-Europe Foundation
ASEM. *See* Asia-Europe Meeting
Asia-Europe Foundation (ASEF), 131
Asia-Europe Meeting (ASEM), 3, 129;
adaption to global changes, 133–134;
centralization of, 130, 131, 133;
collective identity of, 136;
communicative rationality and,
135–137, 138; constructive
engagement, 136, 139; control of, 130,
131–132; early years of, 136; EC and,

129; effectiveness of, 138; flexibility
of, 130, 132–133; as forum tackling
NTS, 137, 139; initiatives of, 137;
institutional design of, 129–133, 136,
138; institutionalization and, 135–136;
interregionalism and, 133, 134, 138;
membership of, 130, 130–131, 136,
137; normative convergence, 135–137;
role of, 134, 135, 138; scope of, 130,
131; shepherd groups of, 131; success
of, 133, 134; summit, 130, 134
Asian Infrastructure Investment Bank
(AIIB), 103
Aso Taro, 88
Australia: competing triads in
policymaking of, 98–100; economy of,
97, 98; foreign policy of, 93, 99, 104;
Japan-PRC relations and, 99, 101;
Japan's relations with, 2, 93–96, 101,
103–104; natural gas of, 93; PRC's
relations with, 2, 93, 96–98, 100, 103,
103–104; regional diplomacy of,
100–103; resources of, 94; trade in, 97;
U.S. and, 101; U.S.-Japan relations and,
103
authoritarianism, 12

balance of power, 6, 111
balance of practices, 111
balance of threat, 6

About Contributors

EDITOR AND CHAPTER 1

Yoneyuki Sugita is professor of history at Osaka University, Japan. His major works include Mayako Shimamoto, Koji Ito, and Yoneyuki Sugita, *Historical Dictionary of Japanese Foreign Policy* (Lanham, MD: The Scarecrow Press, 2015); "U.S. Strategic Preference for Securing Military Bases and Impact of Japanese Financial Community on Constrained Rearmament in Japan, 1945-1954," in Peter N. Stearns ed., *Demilitarization in the Contemporary World* (Champaign, IL: University of Illinois Press, 2013); and *Pitfall or Panacea: The Irony of US Power in Occupied Japan 1945-1952* (New York: Routledge, 2003).

CHAPTER 2

Miyuki Daimaruya is a Project Research Fellow at the Institute for Gender Studies, Ochanomizu University, Japan. Her major works include *"Nisei* Soldiers of the Korean War in 1950s Hollywood Films: From Gender and Ethnic Perspectives," [in Japanese] *Theory of Information Culture,* vol.11 (December 2014); *"Resettlement* Experience of a *Nisei* Woman in *Kiyo's Story,"* [in Japanese] *Journal of Comparative Culture*, vol.106 (March 2013); and "Images of the Korean War in Hollywood from Gender and Ethnic Perspectives," *Journal of the Graduate School of Humanities and Sciences*, Vol.11 (March 2009).

CHAPTER 3

Victor Teo is Assistant Professor at the University of Hong Kong. His field of research is in the International Relations of the Asia-Pacific, with particular emphasis on Sino-Japanese Relations. He is also interested in the issues pertaining to the Global Illicit Political Economy, Maritime Studies and North Korean issues. He is author and contributing editor of four books on Sino-Japanese relations. He can be contacted at victorteo@hku.hk.

CHAPTER 4

Reinhard Drifte is emeritus professor of Newcastle University, UK, and visiting professor at the Universite de Pau, France. His major publications include *The Senkaku/Diaoyu Islands Territorial Dispute between Japan and China. Between the Materialization of the `China Threat` and `Reversing the Outcome of World War II`?* (UNISCI Discussion Papers Complutense University of Madrid), no. 32 (May 2013), http://pendientedemigracion.ucm.es/info/unisci/revistas/UNISCIDP32-1DRIFTE.pdf; Reinhard Drifte, Wilhelm Vosse and Verena Blechinger-Talcott, *Governing Insecurity in Japan: The Domestic Discourse and Policy response* (Sheffield Centre for Japanese Studies/Routledge Series, Sheffield/London 2014); *Japan's security relationship with China since 1989. From balancing to bandwagoning?* (Nissan Institute/Routledge Japanese Studies Series, Oxford/London 2003). For further information see his website www.rfwdrifte.ukgo.com.

CHAPTER 5

David Walton is a Senior Lecturer in International Relations and Asian Studies at the University of Western Sydney (Australia). His recent publications include *New Approaches to Human Security in the Asia Pacific: China, Japan and Australia* William. T. Tow, David Walton and Rikki Kersten (eds.) (London; Ashgate, 2013); *Australia, Japan and Southeast Asia: Early post-war diplomatic initiatives* (New York: Nova Publishers, 2012); 'Australian foreign policy towards Japan: weighing the bureaucratic processes' in William T. Tow and Rikki Kersten (eds). *Bilateral Perspectives on Regional Security: Australia, Japan and the Asia-Pacific Region* (Basingstoke: Palgrave Macmillan, 2012); and 'Australia and Japan: Towards a Full Security Partnership?' Purnendra Jain and Peng Er Lam (eds.) *Japan's Strategic Challenges: The Rise of China, the Hegemonic Decline of the United States and Asian Security*. (Singapore: World Scientific, 2012).

CHAPTER 6

Emilian Kavalski is Associate Professor in Global Studies at the Institute for Social Justice, Australian Catholic University (Sydney). He has held research positions at Aalborg University (Denmark), Academia Sinica (Taiwan), Ruhr University-Bochum (Germany), National Chung-Hsing University (Taiwan), the Rachel Carson Center (Germany), the Killam Postdoctoral Fellowship at the University of Alberta (Canada), and the Andrew Mellon Fellowship at the American Center for Indian Studies (India). Emilian is the author of three books, most recently: *Central Asia and the Rise of Normative Powers: Contextulizing the Security Governance of the European Union, China, and India* (New York: Bloomsbury, 2012) and he is the editor of eight volumes, including *World Politics at the Edge of Chaos: Reflections on Complexity and Global Life* (Albany, NY: State University of New York Press, 2015).

CHAPTER 7

Bart Gaens works as Senior Research Fellow at the Finnish Institute of International Affairs (FIIA) in Helsinki, Finland. He is also Adjunct Professor at the University of Helsinki, and Specially-Appointed Associate Professor at the University of Osaka. He has published extensively on Europe-Asia interregional relations focusing on the ASEM process. Relevant publications include: "ASEM in the wake of the Milan summit", in Wilhelm Hofmeister and Patrick Rueppel (eds), *The Future of Asia-Europe Cooperation*, Konrad-Adenauer Stiftung and European Union (2015); "Interregional relations and legitimacy in global governance: The EU in ASEM", *Asia-Europe Journal* 10: 2-3 (2012, with Juha Jokela); "The development of the EU's Asia strategy with special reference to China and India - Driving forces and new directions", in Bart Gaens; Juha Jokela, and Eija Limnell (eds). *The European Union's Role in Asia: China and India as Strategic Partners*, Ashgate (2009); and *Europe-Asia Interregional Relations – A Decade of ASEM* (Ashgate 2008, editor and co-author).